PRATTL

Peeking Out

Of The

Bedlam

Teri Stricker

Wow! This looks real don't it?

Prattle On - Teri Stricker

Here is the legal hoopla for your perusal

COPYRIGHT © Teri Stricker 2008
License Notes: All rights reserved, including the right to reproduce this book or portions thereof in any form or means whatsoever without prior permission from the author.

Dedication

To my family;
You are huge part of this book
Because you are a huge part of my heart
In these pages is some of the laughter
But we share so much more

THANKS !!! AND STUFF

So my friend says, Teri, you need to write a book. So I says. HUH? So then HE says, well YEAH. So here it is. My book. And stuff. Thanks Jon.

Thanks to several online friends who read this monstrosity I loosely term a book, and told me it was great. If this bombs, I'm sending you the bill. I'd list your names here but if someone finds out which program we are on well, it could get ugly. Do you REALLY want my hate mail?

I'd also like to thank The Academy. No, they nominated me for nothing, I didn't win anything, I just always wanted to say that. Hey, it is MY book after all.

I have to thank my husband of 21 years for BEING my husband of 21 years. I love you head to toe you know. The middle ain't half bad either. Rick Stricker, you married a halfwit, and you've stuck with it. Thank you for not trying to find the other half of the wit, for loving me as I am, warts and all. You also read this whole thing. You should get a medal.

I have to thank YOU, the reader. Without you, I'm just telling myself things I already know. My family has heard all this, they are sick of it.

Lastly, I'd like to thank LIFE. If life wasn't so funny, well, there'd be nothing to write about.

Prattle On - Teri Stricker
PREFACE INTRODUCTION THINGY

Which is it? I don't know. It's one of those, I'm pretty sure.

Hi. I'm Teri. You know, the AUTHOR. This isn't a joke book. It MAY not even be a GOOD book, you have to decide that. It's my thoughts, observations, ramblings and DRIVEL. And I'll digress a LOT.

I'm not famous, so this isn't a "tell all" book. Sorry. I am like, nobody with a capital N. I think that "tell all" stuff is down the aisle. Maybe ask the guy at the counter.

My friend Jon told me I'm funny and I need to write this stuff down, so I'm thinking you should blame HIM. Jon is a good friend, but an online friend. His name may not even be Jon. Doesn't matter, I'm not marrying the man, not buying anything from him, just, you know, talking.

Let us first define "drivel" since this is a whole book of it.

Driv-el (dr-iv-el)

v. driv-eled or driv-elled, driv-el-ing or driv-el-ling, driv-els

1. To slobber; drool.

2. To flow like spittle or saliva.

3. To talk stupidly or childishly.

1. To allow to flow from the mouth.

2. To say (something) stupidly.

1. Saliva flowing from the mouth.

2. Stupid or senseless talk.

I don't drool. Yet. So, it is the talking. So stupid or senseless talk. Except I hope that somewhere along the way will be some humor, maybe a pearl of wisdom or two. I don't know. We shall see.

e

Prattle On - Teri Stricker

Anyway, so I'm not REALLY an author. I'm a singer. I'm a PC Tech. I'm a wife, mother, and grandmother – all that tombstone stuff. So this is just me here, talking. This is just my thoughts, observations, what happened today, that sort of thing. If you run a grammar check you'll crash Microsoft Word although I did try to spell things right. I know, we will say that I am using the colloquial form. Problem solved.

If you know the rules of writing, I'm probably breaking them all. I don't have to follow a plot, it's not a story, and I'm PRETTY sure I don't have to rhyme. This time. Got a dime?

Oh dear. Anyway if this Preface Introduction is to your liking, you may like the rest of the book. If it is NOT, well for heaven's sake put the book down! Don't buy it and then write me about how it sucks. That would be wrong. I've a fragile ego and stuff. I thinj

Chapter One – The Beginning

Wow, here we are at page 1. I'm really doing this. Now isn't that weird. I hate books where you start chapter one and you are on page 32. So this is page one. The ones before this don't count. I was just practicing. I was getting ready for page 1.

So I think it's quite obvious we should start at the beginning. So close your eyes ... wait! If you close your eyes, you can't read, can you? Okay, so don't close your eyes.

We whoosh back to the BEGINNING. I always think of it in capital letters. Doesn't everyone? Now we could talk about the big bang, but unless you are talking about sex, not very funny – so we'll go to Adam and Eve. THEY are a hoot.

Think about it. Adam and Eve had NO children before getting tossed out of Eden on their perfect buttocks. They were PERFECT so obviously it wasn't a problem of fertility, right? Right.

So they sinned DARN fast if you ask me. We all know it was all Satan's fault. We've been blaming him for everything ever since. But think about it, now. Satan was an angel. Going about his duties, whatever angel duties ARE, and God makes Adam and a bunch of critters.

So ole Satan, he says, hmm. He watches all the goings on, but did he try to trick anyone THEN? No. Then God made EVE. Perfect woman, so obviously she was attractive. This is when Satan went. Wait! Wait just a cotton pickin' minute! He gets all these pretty trees and flowers. Ok. Then all the animals. Got it. Now a WOMAN? HEY! I been working my wings off for millennia, did *I* get a woman? No. So down he goes.

So Eve gets tricked into the apple, and boom! OUT! God wasn't any worse than MY father, after all. MY rules MY house. Simple. I'm sure you heard the same thing, right? "You don't want to follow my rules get OUT."

Prattle On - Teri Stricker

Now we go on to the children. Cain and Abel. Remember them? Now, I know Cain was a very bad boy. I do. But I also suspect that Abel was one of them know-it-all pains in the tuckus, don't you? I wouldn't have killed him, but I might have blacked his eye, this is all I'm saying.

So.. Let us move on. For one thing I don't know the names of all of Adam and Eve's children. Lord love a duck, they probably couldn't remember them all EITHER. I have TWO kids and sometimes switch their names when I'm yelling at them.

We rifle through the Bible until we land on a page. Moses. Oh yeah, I remember ole Mose, he was the one who couldn't talk. Told Ole God - I can't talk to people. I freeze up, man, it's a phobia, you know? God sighed and said, so we'll make your brother talk.

Poor Aaron. I mean think about it. Poor guy never had a chance. What would you do if your brother came home and told you he talked to a burning bush? Okay, probably check him into the nearest psycho ward. BUT if he could prove it, now there's a problem. Don't go making God mad, I mean look what happened to Adam and Eve.

And look at NOAH. The man was 600 years old and God says, "Build me an Ark." Oh dear. Now I'm sure the kids helped him, but they HAD to be thinkin' the old man's lost it.

My Dad tells me he's building an ark, well, he lives by water. Maybe I'd just think he wants a big boat. But if he lived in Nebraska, I'd be wondering about his sanity, I think. Yep. The old man's lost it.

But then, they NEEDED that ark. So it's a good darn thing they didn't find that psycho ward. Otherwise, well, this extremely intelligent book wouldn't be written would it? And you, dear reader, wouldn't be here to read it.

Then we fast forward a LOT to Jesus. Very cool dude. I mean look at that HAIR. That's trendsetting hair, my friends! He was right out of the sixties wasn't he? Now that I mention it, so was the LOVE talk. Well, maybe not. Sixties love was a lot messier, and definitely not approved by the BIBLE. So, okay, no sixties love.

So we covered the beginning, and tied it up with a bow. We skipped the middle. This isn't because the middle isn't interesting, mind you. But, really, just how long do you want this book to be?

This ends chapter one, so it's a good time to go to the bathroom, if that isn't where you are reading this in the first place.

Prattle On - Teri Stricker
Chapter Two – The Characters

These are short ass chapters but it makes the slow readers feel they've accomplished more. I think. My son gets mad at me because I read so fast. I've been devouring books for like, 35 years. I should have sped up by now, I'd think. I love to read, it's this writing thing that worries me.

Okay, come back to now. There's plenty about our own times to laugh at.

For example in New Jersey, on Halloween 2008, a kid was sent home for coming to school dressed as Jesus Christ. I saw the picture; he did a great job on his costume.

So the ghosts, goblins, Satan himself, they were okay, but Jesus had to go home. The article said it wasn't for religious reasons. It was that it was so disruptive. DISRUPTIVE? Why is Jesus disruptive? George Bush is disruptive. Obama, McCain, they are disruptive. Cause arguments aplenty. But JESUS? Apparently I'm missing something. Ole Jesus is a criminal all over again. Poor guy can't get a break can he?

Politics, I avoid. It is only funny when someone ELSE talks about it. Like Jay Leno. He can talk about politics. He's good at it.

So politics is out, unless of course, I change my mind in another chapter. You never know, I'm a woman after all.

So, where to start? Well, I have a family. It's that perfect nuclear family. Mom, Dad, Girl, Boy. What could go wrong?

Evidently, a LOT.

MOM is a halfwit, did I mention that? Oh yeah in the THANKS, that you probably didn't read. Actually, I shouldn't lie, I'm not a halfwit. I'm quite smart sometimes, it just that these weird thoughts whirl about in my head. Like this whole book. Can you imagine having me for a mother? It's amazing my kids aren't in prison sharpening their axes or something. Anyway, I figure you will get to know me if you keep reading my book, so you know, we'll just move on.

Prattle On - Teri Stricker

DAD is a genius. No, I'm not being sarcastic he really is. IQ is through the roof. He actually UNDERSTANDS the theory of relativity. It's replacing the toilet roll he can't handle. Oh dear, he's reading this. I love you honey!

GIRL. Lord love a duck how to describe GIRL. Well she is a girl. Let's get that up front. I want no one believing my GIRL is a BOY. That would be confusing. And wrong. And stuff. She did the Barbie dolls and all, and then when she was done, somehow Barbie was EVIL. No kidding. Barbie went from way cool to I don't know who, Satan's sister or something. GIRL, just you know, move on, ok?

BOY. Yes, he really is a boy. In fact he was ALL boy growing up. Well except when my GIRL and her girlfriends decided to put him in makeup. He was amazingly patient with them. No black eyes. Just let them do their thing, and then washed it off. I think he scrubbed too hard, he was missing some skin.

BOY also had very original ways of getting himself hurt. He couldn't just fall out of a tree like a NORMAL person, oh no! He was CHASED out of the tree by a Squirrel. Evidently the squirrel couldn't take a BOY squirrelier than he was.

MOM, DAD, GIRL and BOY will probably be all over this book, so you know, get used to them. I have to deal them out to you a little at a time. Not because they are scary, it's just how my mind works. When it works.

I'll bet you think - this woman is crazy. Mad as a hatter. Well I'm not. No really, no white vans, chasing me down the street or anything. No fancy jacket with extra long sleeves. That might just be because I'm harmless. No bloody axe, no shot gun. I don't even stand on podiums and run for public office. I just talk, that's all.

I'd worry right now about losing the theme, or the flow, but since there ISN'T any, I can just go on.

I think.

Anyway it's probably time to get something to eat, or do that potty thing, or answer your spouse who you've been ignoring this whole chapter, so we'll do another chapter. Makes it look like a real book that way.

Prattle On - Teri Stricker
Chapter Three – Family Stuff

See? Here we are at chapter three. And you're still here. And they call ME crazy. I'm wondering what that says about you? Well never mind, here we are.

Now, if you read the THANKS way back when you opened this book, you know I am ONLINE a lot. For anyone living under a rock, or otherwise uninformed, ONLINE means on the Internet. And I meet folks in chat rooms. That sort of thing. No wild romances though, I'm still on my honeymoon here in the real world.

Some of my online friends have read this. Satin says I sound like a rambling half crazy woman, for example. So, we're on the right track I think, I sound like me. That's a relief. Sounding like someone else would be polygamy. Wait, no, that's multiple wives. That would REALLY bad, since I'm not even into women.

Well, it's bad, sounding like someone else, and then people sue you for all your money and stuff. And since I'm broke, that would be bad.

Caz, another online friend, she just keeps asking for more of the book. That's GOOD, right? I DID warn you back at the PREFACE INTRODUCTION that this book is just, well ME. Talking. Prattling. If you are still here, I guess that's ok. If I'm talking to myself, well, that's not new either.

Anyway, where were we? Oh yeah, that's what I was deciding. Let's talk about THEM. Comics like THEM. You know why? THEY are stupid. It's true, people are stupid. Not YOU, of course YOU bought my book, so you are obviously one of US, not THEM.

THEY say things like "If your friend jumped off a cliff, would you do that too?" Wait, that was my mother. But I like it. How do you answer that anyway? My mother never liked my answers. "Well WHY did he jump off a cliff? I mean, was he on a bungee? Was he being chased by a bear? WHY?"

Don't you hate that? My son did that to me all the time. I used to tell him he could be replaced by a button that didn't work when he frustrated me. THEN he'd ask me things like "what color button?". I was a great Mom; by the way, he is still alive.

THEY also told my brother if he did something too much he'd grow hair on his palms. Nope, wrong, that was my mother too. Hmmm, so I guess we're talking about my mom. This can't be good. All I can say is he never had hairy palms so, either she was wrong or he listened. If he DID listen, it'd have been a first. Well, according to her anyway.

I didn't tell my son things like that. For one thing, he was much too smart to try that stuff on, and for another, I didn't have the heart. I can just picture a poor kid staring at his hands, waiting for the hair.

I can't tell you our family motto, because it comes from a book I'd have to go and find out how to get permission to use a phrase from. Suffice it to say it is a warm and fuzzy motto. Why we have a family motto, I don't know. I'm afraid to think what the motto would be for the family I grew up in would have been. Probably "Stop That!" or "Put that down!"

The other thing DAD and I said over and over and over was "If you don't do it right you are going to have problems." I'm sure GIRL and BOY repeat it in their sleep. They've certainly heard it enough. Whether it sunk in remains to be seen. I think all your hard work shows up when they are about 30. Maybe 50. Okay, no idea.

You think I am kidding? I hope I'm not. Because right this minute it looks like they didn't hear a WORD. And when I was their age, I was the same. Not exactly the same, of course, but I'm sure my mother thought all her teachings had failed. They just took a while to grow that's all. So if you are worried, don't panic. If they don't wind up in jail, count your blessings.

Okay, now I finally thought of some THEY things, but this has turned out to be more a FAMILY chapter so, I think it's time to CHAPTER again. Are you ready? Me neither. There's the cliff. JUMP!

Prattle On - Teri Stricker
Chapter Four – THEY

Okay, are you okay? See? That cliff wasn't big at all, was it? I hope I didn't scare you too bad. Stephen King is the horror guy, I'd hate to tread on his territory or something.

So here we are at the THEY chapter. I DID warn you I ramble. I think.

THEY say you mold your children. THEY obviously don't have children. MY children were who they are today. Oh I taught them things, tried to teach them self control and all. But you can't MOLD them. They aren't clay. They're people. Little tiny people. Well, mine are both bigger than me now, but they started out little. Thank God. I mean, I look at my son and go, where did THAT come from?

GIRL still has the same smile. She is still that little girl. Oh she's a more mature form of that little girl, but she didn't become ME after all. That's probably a good thing. She has her own ideas, her own STUFF. Shoot she even has her own kids now. I should ask her if she still hates Barbie.

BOY started laughing about the time most babies smile, and he's been doing it ever since. I didn't have TIME to teach him life was funny back then, he already KNEW it. He didn't become me, he didn't become his father, he became HIMSELF. So THEY are obviously full of crap on the molding thing.

THEY say "a stitch in time saves nine". HUH? I get what a stitch is, I've sewn like, hems… and time is obvious. So I'm with the meanings of the WORDS but string them like that, and I think THEY are nuttier than me. Saves nine WHAT? Maybe that made sense once? I don't know. I think maybe we lost the nine. Maybe that's it. Find the nine and we won't be lost anymore. It's a theory anyway.

THEY say "the grass is always greener on the other side". But it's not. Standing on the hill … it's all pretty much the same green. And even if one side is greener because the sun was there more, well, it's not necessarily the OTHER side is it? It might be the side we're on. If it IS the side we're on, then the grass is DEFINITELY not greener on the OTHER side is it?

Prattle On - Teri Stricker

I never ran for greener. I've been married 21 years, and I'm telling you grass is grass. I've moved a few times too. Grass is still grass. Well in Kentucky it's blue, they say, but you know, when I drove through Kentucky, I didn't see much grass. I saw a lot of rock. Lovely rock, but it wasn't grass. The rest area grass, that was green. That's all I got.

Even in the meaning they came up with, grass is still grass. I mean, really. I know people who have been married four and five times. How many times before you figure out, grass is grass? If you don't fix what's wrong with your commitment gear, or your compromise gear, well, then you are going to get married a LOT. Or maybe it's another gear, I don't know, maybe it's the choosing the spouse gear that's broken. You get the idea. Obviously, I could go on all day, you've probably noticed that about me. But I'll move on.

THEY say truth is how you perceive it. In other words, it's different for each person. HUH? My math teacher would never buy that. I don't care what you do, $2+2=4$. If you think it is 8, well, you are wrong. If you think going out and killing people is OK, well you are probably in prison. But if you are NOT, you're still wrong. Truth isn't malleable. When I had a true or false question on a test it was true or it was false. I got red checkmarks, I know. My teacher didn't write.. "well, it's true to YOU".

Multiple choice was the same. It wasn't really a CHOICE was it? You got a big red mark if you didn't circle the one they wanted you to circle. Life is just the same. If you went out to party and tell your spouse you went shopping. Friends, that's a LIE. This isn't a difficult concept but THEY are stupid. I told you that in the last chapter. Right?

THEY say "an apple a day keeps the doctor away". OK, but what if you NEED a doctor? Last I knew apples didn't prevent many diseases. I should maybe ask my doctor what he has against apples anyway. The flip side of this must be if I don't eat that apple the doctor will be at my door? I haven't noticed this problem. That's a good thing, doctors are expensive.

Prattle On - Teri Stricker

THEY do have a few good ones. Like "a person is known by the company he keeps". Boy are YOU in trouble. Look who you are with. Me. Perhaps you need a therapist. No, I can't recommend any, I spend my life avoiding them. I'm happy. I prefer not to delve into 101 reasons not to be happy. I should write a book on how to be happy. Except, I don't know exactly how to do it. Not hitting your thumb with that hammer might be a good start though.

THEY say "ask me no questions I'll tell you no lies". So, why ARE we listening to THEM at all? I mean. Jeezopete already, you just told me you are a bold faced liar. How stupid am I anyway? Don't answer that. Oh wait, you lie, go ahead and answer that.

THEY say "all good things come to those who wait". THEY are totally nuts aren't they?

I wait at the doctor's office, and that's rarely good. I wait in line at Walmart, and well, eventually I do get OUT of there, but I'm pretty sure that's not what they mean. So maybe I should quit my job and go sit in the park and wait. The problem is some police officer is going to think I'm a homeless person or something, and tell me to move on. So, where to wait? And what are ALL good things? I mean you might love liver, so liver is a good thing to you. Personally, I can't stand the stuff.

Oh but wait. . You waited for "all good things" and maybe you got them? Well don't look now but...

THEY say "All good things come to an end.". Oh my GOD! So we waited for who knows HOW long for "all good things" and a week later they're GONE? Okay, this doesn't sound like the best plan to me.

I think we're right back to having to work for our good things. Dang. They still might come to an end I guess, but at least you won't be bored out of your skull waiting for them.

THEY say "Blood will out.". Um, only if you make a hole in the skin. The skin was designed to keep that blood in. If your blood is coming out, you might want to find a band-aid or something. Of course the common definition is actually about heritage. But you know that's a crock too.

I mean what about the American Dream? Ghetto kids make good, all that? So THEY are wrong yet again. Well you know THEY really need to sit down and think things out before THEY spout this stuff, don't you think?

THEY say "barking dogs seldom bite". Okay I have to agree with that one. It's hard to bite while you are actually barking. You have to shut up for minute to do that, I think. I THINK. I haven't actually bitten anyone. Maybe I should try that on my husband.

On second thought, that's probably not a great idea. First, I LIKE my husband, so why would I want to bite him? Second, he might decide I've gone whole crazy and find a nice room for me with rubber walls and crayons. I mean if YOUR wife got down on the floor, barked like a dog and BIT you, wouldn't you?

This THEY chapter is kind of fun. It might end up kind of long. I hope you have a bookmark or something. Maybe you should look up and see if dinner is burning or something. I'd hate to be to blame for your house burning down.

THEY say "Close only counts in horseshoes and hand-grenades.". To tell you the truth, I've said it too. But is it TRUE? I mean if a bomb is close, it will still cause damage right? It's not a horseshoe OR a hand grenade.

THEY say "Curiosity killed the cat. Satisfaction brought it back". Okay what was the cat's name, Lazarus? Curiosity might kill the cat, I can go with that. Accidentally put your head in a guillotine, and oops! But the coming back thing, I haven't seen that. Dead is pretty much dead.

THEY say "Don't cross a bridge until you come to it." Good idea and all, but HOW do you cross a bridge you haven't come to? I suppose you could try, if you think you can fly. But no, you STILL have to get to that bridge. Of course if you are flying, you don't really NEED the bridge do you?

THEY say "He who hesitates is lost." But if he's hesitating, it might be to look at a map?

Oh wait, it's HE, that's a guy, guys don't look at maps, they fold them. They don't ask for directions either, so I guess they just KNOW. So, if you start out for Florida from Michigan and wind up in Alaska that was just a side trip, right?

THEY say "Honesty is the best policy.". I like this one, I DO. But you go right ahead and tell your wife her butt is fat, see what happens.

"No honey, those pants don't you're your ass look fat, your ass IS fat."

You'll be very intimate with the frying pan, I'm pretty sure. I am, in fact, a lousy liar. Never ask me if you look fat. I'll lie, all right, you just won't believe me.

Okay, so I've overdone the THEY chapter, but it was fun. Nobody's actually going to READ this anyway are they? So go put out the fire that started because you were just going to read this short chapter. I'm sorry. I really am. Call it Cajun, that always works.

I can't wait to see what the next chapter is. No, really, I have no clue what it is. I told you, I'm just talking. Ready? Yeah, me neither. Maybe we should think this out. Last time, after all, we jumped off a cliff.

Okay, deep breath…. Here we go!!!!!!!

Prattle On - Teri Stricker
Chapter Five – Moving South and Stuff

Wow Chapter five. I'm really rather impressed with myself. My friend Jon, you know, the instigator of this travesty? He just read through the last four. I knew he was nuts already though, I mean, he talks to me. Anyway he claims it's great. What does he know? He doesn't even have a last name. But I'll take it anyway.

Meanwhile we need a topic. I know, I'll tell you about my move to the south. Yeah, that could work. Maybe. What the hell, it can't be worse than the last four chapters, can it?

Let me explain a bit how this move came about first, I guess. I was born in Michigan. My parents, both of them, were born in Michigan. They named me Teri Jo. Any further north and we'd be in CANADA and they name me Teri Jo. Really, were they PLANNING on me to be an outcast?

Anyway, so, I lived in Michigan from birth until I joined the Navy, and then after the Navy, I went back. I'll explain the Navy crap later. This is the moving to the south crap.

So if I was titling this chapter I guess I'd name it, "Moving To The South and Stuff". Catchy. I like it. Now I have to think up catchy titles for the last FOUR chapters. That sounds an awful lot like work.

Anyway, where was I? Oh yeah moving. Well it all started with ONLINE. I know, I know, I'm kind of addicted to ONLINE. You may have noticed.

There was this program run by a guy who claimed he was a producer. I'm a singer, remember? Anyway, I wasn't looking to be produced, but we were doing a lot of fun stuff, songwriting classes, and voice lessons, and just, you know STUFF.

So this guy, who shall remain nameless because even I am not stupid enough to name people who probably don't want to be named, was going to have a benefit for someone.

In Nashville. Yeah, the one in Tennessee. Hey, there could be one in Idaho, I don't know.

Prattle On - Teri Stricker

After three cancellations of this benefit, I said to DAD, okay, screw the benefit. I want to see Nashville before I die. And DAD, my genius husband, said "Great idea". He's smart, I told you. So we went.

Well, what happened is we had the week of our lives. I fell in love with Nashville and the South in general. These people TALK. I fit right in. Don't get me wrong, you say hi to someone in Michigan, they say hi back, or nod and smile. But in the SOUTH you have a CONVERSATION. This is where I was meant to be, you see that, right?

Anyway, so we went home after a glorious week, and after a little dreaming about moving, settled back into Michigan life.

Then GIRL's husband, we'll call him, let's see SLSIL. That stands for Silly Little Son In Law. Yes. He knows. He dubbed me MOMIL – Mean Old Mother In Law, so we're quite even. Anyway he started talking about moving to Virginia. DAD got into the act, and they are now looking at real estate and demographics, and you know, stuff.

So now MOM, that's me, pipes in with "What the hell is in Virginia? If we're going to make some huge move, why not go to Nashville? We already know we love it there."

Anyway, long story short (yeah I know, kinda too late isn't it?) we moved to Tennessee. It was very exciting, and a little scary, and we did it.

Now, I must explain that moving north to south is kinda like moving to a different country. EVERYTHING is different. The people are more talkative like I said, there's the accent, and you can't find a damn thing. There are hills everywhere. You need good directions because the stores HIDE from you.

No, I'm not kidding they HIDE. It's the hills. Nothing is easy to see from the road. And things close at ridiculous times. The bank closes at 4. They claim they all are on EST. So you are trying to tell me banks in California close at 2? I don't know if I buy all that.

Anyway so we pull up the moving van to the house, and we are moving in. That's just what you do, when you are moving, right? You do it too, right? Whew! Good I thought it was just us.

So the neighbor on the right side comes over and stands in the yard. Introduces himself, very nice. Then he says. "So, you moving in?"

Oh my sweet Lord, it was a Bill Engvall moment if I ever heard one. And you can't DO it! You can't. You can't say what pops in your head because this person lives NEXT DOOR. You don't know how long he's gonna live there either. And he might have a shotgun. Which, face it, is the ONLY time you think of great lines, isn't it?

But, YOU, I'll tell, I mean, you aren't going to go tell him, right? So what I wanted to say, what made me bite my lip until it bled, was, "Nope! See, we came to rob the place. Then we seen they don't have no stuff. So we thought, we'd bring them some STUFF."

But remember, I did NOT say it. I had control and stuff. Now, a neighbor from the OTHER side of me comes over. We're still hauling stuff. BIG moving van. He says;

"Lived here long?"

My poor lip. I thought it was never going to be the same. You've come with me through four chapters, and I think you might know how hard it is for me to SHUT THE HELL UP. So, my poor lip.

Anyway, I can tell YOU. You are trustworthy right? Besides, this book isn't actually going to GO anywhere anyway. So, what I nearly killed myself NOT saying was, "Boy where you been? We've been here 20 years!"

Except later, I realized, he might have believed me. That house next door had apartments, and the tenants come and go rather quickly. So. He might have just moved in himself.

So, anyway we get everything into the house. You know the drill, boxes everywhere. It's now midnight, so you throw mattresses on the floor, dig out the bedding and crash.

Except. I'm a smoker. So I went out in the back yard to smoke. From the darkness I hear. "HOWDY!"

After I picked myself off the ground, I discover it is the neighbor behind my house, so I say "Howdy" right back. I'm adaptable and stuff. So I go to the back fence to talk, being polite.

And then he says. "You can call me Bubba."

Oh my GOD. It's HIM! Bubba! I've heard about him all my life! He shot the jukebox! He sees UFOS and stuff! But he didn't look a thing like I imagined. For one thing, he was skinny. He had gray hair. Distinguished looking even.

All my Bubba dreams were shattered.

Okay. That's the move. I'm not going to whine about how many days every muscle ached, or how GIRL and SLSIL and DAD and I drove each other batty figuring out where things should go.

But in the interest of keeping the chapters short, since I can't have you burning down the house reading my STUFF, I think it's time to chapter again.

We've been through this five times now. We're getting pretty good at chaptering you and I, aren't we? So brace yourself for the Chapter ride, and we'll just DO it.

One ……. Two……

Prattle On - Teri Stricker
Chapter Six – South Versus North

THREE!

Ha! Fooled you didn't I? Yeah I know, cheap. But I want to keep it interesting, after all. I can't have you getting bored on me already. I mean this is only chapter six.

As I said, the North and the South are completely different in more than just the weather. The PEOPLE are different.

For example, down here, they will talk to you THREE YARDS AWAY. That is like yards, the ones that come with houses, not yards, the 36 inches one. So there is a lot of hollering across the neighborhood during the day. There's a REASON they have a distance called a holler. Not fights, mind you they are just TALKING. This took a little getting used to.

You do NOT say hello unless you have time to talk. Because you WILL talk. It is not hard to pull away because they are boring, it's hard to pull away because they are NOT boring.

From the Walmart Greeter to the lady looking at the same stuff in the same aisle, they are quite willing to have a conversation. And they are willing to give advice too. The only people that are NOT willing to help you in Walmart are the people who actually WORK there.

THESE souls are nowhere to be found. This is the same, north, south, east or west, as far as I can see, and don't think I'm booing Walmart. I'm not. I'm simply there at the wrong time, all the time. I am sure this is it. All the big stores are like this. I can't find someone who works at a place no matter where I go. So, I think they see me coming and run.

You know "Oh my God, it's THAT woman." I probably can't blame them. I mean, even my husband looks at me funny from time to time.

Prattle On - Teri Stricker

I've gotten demanding in my middle years. When I was young, I'd wait and wait for help somewhere. Now I demand some service. This doesn't come from becoming more selfish, to be honest. It comes from having worked in customer service for 25 years and thinking I should get as good as I give. I do back flips for my customers, go to great lengths to help them, so I expect the same when I am the customer.

No matter where you go there are people, talking, always talking. I love this. I am in love with the south. It's as if I've lived in the wrong place all my life, and suddenly, I'm home!

But there are many things I have had to learn, and probably there are more surprises to come. For instance, "Bless your heart!".

This phrase is used in different ways. The way we yanks KNOW about is in commiseration or an otherwise nice manner. "Poor thing lost her husband last week, bless her heart."

But, that's not the only way. Oh no. You also hear "She's a few toys short in the attic, bless her heart." They are very polite when they insult you, you see. A holdover from the old south, perhaps. I don't know. All I know is you gotta listen when you hear that phrase to know iffin you is good or you is bad.

The first thing you have to do when you hit the south is SLOW DOWN. "Slow down son, I can't understand a WORD". Listen to the southern accents you've heard. Slow drawl. Their MINDS ain't slow, you'll be in a world of hurt iffin you assume that.

I think it's the heat. The heat forced folks to take it easy in the heat of the day, and their speech reflects it. This ain't all bad friends. I'm sure there are plenty of ulcers down here, but I bet it's less than up north. We yanks are rushing everywhere and everything. We rush to go to the beach for pity's sake. Of course, summer's so short, I suppose we have to, summer could be over before we get there!

They FIX to do things. "I'm fixin' to go to the store." They use words like "iffin'" but I love it. I pick some of it up, it's just too fun not to.

Ya'll know about rednecks. But the other side is the good ole boys. Now this camp is a little different. They too, have cars on blocks, but the cars change, because they actually know how to fix them. They don't have the rusting wrecks, they cycle them through. They work hard, and they play hard.

So as a group, they are friendly, and warm, and outgoing. How could you not love it? Well, you know, plenty don't. For one thing, when you are trying to get something done, it can be downright infuriating.

Now, my neighbors, they change, especially at the apartment house next door. They have all the flavors there. You have the clean cut college kids, you have the rednecks, good ole boys, etc. And sometimes they drive me crazy.

One of the apartments the door and steps is next to my driveway. I am forever cleaning up cigarette butts and all out of my driveway. One tenant attracted all the stray dogs to my yard by dumping her leftovers IN MY DRIVEWAY.

I've never in my life seen someone do this. I was dumbstruck. And some of the things she dumped were, well, they didn't look very appetizing at all. The first time I thought maybe it was a fight. You know, husband mouths off that dinner don't taste so good, and wife says "FINE!" tosses the food out the door in a huff.

But oh NO, this was just LIFE. Now, I'm very careful, dealing with folks. They might have shotguns, and besides that, I'm kinda small you see. Getting in a fist fight, is not one of the smartest things I could do in life, you see what I'm sayin'?

So I stood in the driveway one day, surrounded by stray dogs eating the leftovers she'd just thrown, and I yelled real loud to DAD. "You know darlin', someone needs to tell these folks they don't LIVE in the HILLS no more! Folks ain't partial to having garbage thrown in their yards here in the big city!"

Prattle On - Teri Stricker

I was gambling that she'd hear me since only the screen door was closed up there, and I was also gambling she wouldn't come out and dump some food on my HEAD.

Anyway, it worked, the daily dog food extravaganza ended. But that wasn't the end. Our next hurdle was THE FENCE PISSER.

I kid you not, ok? I couldn't make this stuff up. This guy in the rear apartment was peeing on my fence. Daily. It's like the 10 steps inside to the bathroom was just too far to go or something. (These are not large apartments). I was constantly hosing down that fence, with a very disgusted look on my face.

So one day DAD catches him.. sees the top of his head from our deck and sees the fence changing color. So he yells out "go piss on a tree and leave the fence alone!"

This guy says "I ain't!"

The look on DAD's face was priceless, I assure you. So he says "Well do your ain'ting over at that tree over there." I would have said "yonder" myself. I do so like to fit in.

At any rate, the fence pissing stopped, thank goodness. I spent the rest of the summer trying to clean that fence, but I really think the smell just wore away finally.

I am a farmer's daughter. Sort of. Yes folks, Michigan has farms. My father had a small family farm; it wasn't anything to toot your horn over, just some chickens, pigs, a cow, some goats, that stuff. So I ain't all girly over farms. But there's a place for them, and it ain't in a city neighborhood, right?

The neighbors on the other side of me, they were nice folks. We helped each other now and again as neighbors are supposed to do. But they had ducks. And a pig. Now, being a farmer's daughter and all I made the mistake of asking when butchering time was in these parts.

Oh my dear, not the best question. "These are my BABIES!" You know, they didn't even eat the duck eggs. So here I am in the middle of town next to 6 ducks and a pot bellied pig named "Mo".

The day before cleaning day was the worst, the smell wafting across the yard to me. But mostly I didn't mind, and you HAVE to see the humor in the situation don't you? Every day she'd be out there, talking to her babies. Baby talk. Why not baby talk, after all, it's not like you are going to teach them the wrong way to talk. For those of you not "in the know", animals don't talk like in the cartoons.

Mo was a sweet, huge pig. When it got cold they took the whole .. farm into their basement. Can't have the babies getting cold, can you? I'd hate to think what that basement had to smell like when they moved. I didn't actually see folks going in there in bio hazard suits, but boy they should have!

Anyway, that's the south that I live in, my little corner of it anyway. You know, I think we're going to have to chapter again. I don't know what Chapter Seven is going to do for us. This one was informative though, wasn't it?

Maybe?

Anyway, so on to the next one. You probably need a break, I know I do. My coffee is like, empty. The last four paragraphs I have been picking it up to drink and getting nothing. Yep, definitely time to chapter.

Prattle On - Teri Stricker
Chapter Seven - Nashville

Wow, look how far we've come. It's amazing. You ain't left me lying in a dusty corner, and I'm still here. I really feel we are becoming friends. What on earth you see in me, I've no clue, but hey, I'll take it.

Maybe it's time to tell you a little more about myself. First I don't live IN Nashville, I live about an hour away. So my neighbor tales aren't Nashvillian tales. I don't want you wandering Nashville looking for ducks and pigs. I'm pretty sure (but only PRETTY sure) you won't find them.

I moved down here so I could get up to Nashville when I wanted to. You may have noticed I love people. People are wonderful critters aren't they? And they are usually house-trained too. I love to watch them. There are a few that maybe should be watched behind bars, like in a zoo, but so far I've not been harmed in my safaris.

Nashville isn't ALL about music; there are malls and things just like anywhere else. But down on Broadway, where the tourists come, is the absolute best people watching ever. I don't bring binoculars, because that worries the natives. It would worry me too, I suppose. I speak like I am not one of them, but I am. Really, I've got the two legs and the two arms and the beady little eyes. All the features of the classic humanoid. So I guess I am a wonderful critter too.

So when you drive I-65 into Nashville, the landmark that tells you that you have arrived in Nashville is the AMSouth building. We call it the bat cave. It has two little towers sticking up and the shape just makes me think.. Batman's cave. Although I believe my husband actually came up with the term. Yes DAD can come up with some interesting things too. Although later, we found out this wasn't an original thought, everyone thinks of it that way.

Prattle On - Teri Stricker

The Nashville interstates all merge, so the exit numbers make no sense until you've driven it a zillion times. We haven't. So, we get lost. A lot. But it's also this big circle, so if you keep driving that circle, sooner or later you'll find an exit that will get you where you need to be. I think. You're just, you know, late.

So we take the Broadway exit and here we go. I'm not going to give detailed directions; I don't even drive, so I did that you might just wind up in Mississippi or something.

The first hurdle is parking. There is plenty, but you have to be careful. I like the ones where you pay the machines, because you know it's not some guy that don't even own the lot taking your money and then you still get a ticket. There's also parking garages and all, but I'm sure if you've made it this far, you are intelligent enough to find a parking place.

Then you walk down to where it is all happening. The afternoon crowd is not quite as big as the weekend night crowds, but they are just as interesting. The first folks you meet, whether you want to or not are the panhandlers. They are everywhere.

The law doesn't say panhandling is wrong, but they can go to jail for lying. That don't stop them from lying, I'm sure, but I'm just saying, that's the law.

Anyway, they look poor and needy, and probably make more in a year than I do. But they ARE interesting. In the interest of not going to jail, they usually don't tell stories at all, just hold out their cup or whatever and ask for money.

The funniest was a woman. She always had a bag in her hand. McDonalds bag or something. And she's lost. She don't want your money, she claims, just directions. And she'll follow you unless you walk fast.

The first time we saw her was when we came down on a house hunting expedition. We outpaced her and all was well. Then about 4 months later we ran into her again. She is STILL lost. STILL wants directions. And of course is still trying to follow us to talk.

Prattle On - Teri Stricker

I said "Honey, maybe you need to buy you a map. You've been lost a long time!" DAD just gave me a look and sped me up.

There are real homeless people, too, there's just no way of telling which are which. So now here we are on Broadway, in Nashville, Tennessee. In the summer on a Saturday night, and it is absolutely SEETHING with people.

There is no way at all to walk down those sidewalks without brushing against someone. It's very clean. The law is quite visible, and so there really isn't a lot of trouble in the street. Between the panhandlers are the street singers. They have their guitar case (or you know something, anyway) out for tips and they sound good. Unlike the panhandlers they are working for them though. Music wafts out of all the clubs, most have big clean front windows, and the bands have their backs to you.

You see a lot of ass. But you hear a lot of good music. Unlike our visions of Nashville, it ain't all country. Some nights it's hard to FIND a club with a country band. It's a songwriter town, Nashville. It's not so much a PERFORMING town. The artists ain't making half what you think they are. Not those in the clubs. They're working for tips, just like those street singers are. So you go ahead and drop a dollar in their bucket, or guitar case, they are well worth it.

I sing ONLINE, like I said. Unless you manage to convince folks you are good enough to play those Broadway clubs, singing in a band doesn't pay much. And then I'm not certain they are making that much either. I sing ONLINE. I don't have to pay for gas or drinks that way. They do it for the love of performing, and the hope you can move up to them bigger clubs. In Michigan the clubs paid the band and took a cover or whatever to pay for it. It doesn't work like that here.

DAD plays keys and is in a small, just starting out country band, this is how I know.

Anyway, I digress. Well, I've digressed all through this book so far, so that shouldn't surprise you a whole lot, right? Right.

Prattle On - Teri Stricker

So here you are on the sidewalks, with the lights a'blinkin' and the people a'seethin' and you know, stuff.

The ones you may have heard of even if you ain't been near Tennessee, they are there. Like Tootsies. Don't miss Tootsies. It's a landmark, a hallowed hall, for a reason.

Tootsies is a dive. I think they work to keep it that way. It's tiny, the stage downstairs in the window couldn't fit a six piece band if you tried. But it ROCKS. I don't know what the wallpaper looks like because pictures are hung everywhere. There's a picture of everyone you have ever heard of on these walls and some you ain't heard of yet, and some you never will hear of.

The music is LOUD and it's great. I don't care who is up there on the stage, it's great. So go there. On the crowded nights you work your way back out to the street before long, because it's HOT. It's summer, and you're packed like sardines, after all.

Back to the people, the seething people. Yes, I like that word, I'm glad you noticed!

Elvis is everywhere. You know he's dead, I know he's dead, but there he is anyway. Several versions, but mostly the young, hot Elvis. You may see a singing star in that crowd, but it ain't likely. They've been known to show up and be singing in one of those clubs though, you just never know.

Seething people, Teri, jeez, can't you stay on topic?

Tourists and locals all seething together. You will see Bubba in several forms, you'll see ladies in chic outfits and women that look like maybe they forgot to brush their hair today. You'll see young college kids seething next to Ma and Pa Kettle. They are all there, and they are all wonderful.

Here, let's press against the wall here and listen.

"Hey, are we anywhere near Tootsies yet?"

"Wow cowboy hats for $5 you wanna go see?"

"That girl is HOT." "Where?" "Right... aw she's GONE!"

All accents you will hear, even a few languages. But look at them. Most are smiling. Some are awestruck. Count me among the awestruck. It still does it to me. Many have cameras and people are amazingly polite about getting out of the way for someone to take a shot. These are HAPPY sardines my friend.

"Is that George Jones?"

You look wildly around, and you see him. Nope, it's not George, but a very good look alike, at first glance. You may see a Minnie Pearl, as well, complete with price tag.

Wander on down the side streets there are more clubs. Including BB Kings, where I've seen him in the doorway. Wild Horse is where a lot of big acts get booked (also at BB's for that matter. There's also a Coyote Ugly. The comments made passing there could make a trucker blush.

Amid all the clubs where bands are performing are Karaoke clubs as well. But I tell you most of those Karaoke singers are GOOD. Now they do get worse as the folks get drunker and braver, of course, but early on, it's rare to hear anything bad.

Stop and TALK to people. They don't bite. We talk to all the street singers, and if someone asks where something is and they actually know, they'll tell you. They're NICE people. Well, some of them will give you directions because they THINK they know where it is, but they MEAN well.

The locals know the best places to eat, for the least cash, all that good stuff. It's just not always easy to pick out the locals from the tourists. This is the SOUTH honey. Just go into one of the zillion gift shops and ASK.

Most of these folks weren't born here either, just like me they came down and fell in love with it all. It's a town of dreamers, but it's also a town of real live people. Just trying to make a living, just like everyone else. I mean, really, not EVERYONE in Nashville is trying to break into the music business.

I know, this chapter wasn't so funny, I'm sorry. But how could I ramble without touching on my favorite place in the world? I mean really, could YOU? Well second favorite place, I guess. The first favorite place is in a crowd of the people you love, isn't it? Don't matter if it's in the middle of a corn field or even a junk yard. It's who is there.

Anyway, I think we gotta chapter. No, I'm NOT kidding, this chapter is LONG. I mean how long can you sit on that toilet anyway? Your legs are asleep, admit it. So, time to chapter. I'm afraid of running out of inventive ways to do this. Might be a short book!

Let's see what we come up with for Nine. Sound like a plan? And, friend, don't forget to wash your hands.

Prattle On – Teri Stricker
Chapter Eight – I get in trouble

You know, I couldn't resist. I mean, all this chaptering is such serious business. And do we really CARE what chapter we are on? No. They are just convenient breaks, usually by topic, or where you are in the story, or, something.

I should start naming them Chapter umptyfrat. Wouldn't THAT just thrill a publisher? Yeah, I know. I've been told I'm just not right. Daily. It's okay. I'm happy, so maybe just not right is a GOOD thing. You think?

Okay so we are about to hit on one of my pet peeves. So try and remember, however I rant, I LIKE you. DAD hid my bloody axe years ago, so you are quite safe. Anyway my pet peeve is . . .

DRUMROLL … Okay, is it me or does that drummer suck? Okay okay, don't hurt yourself, I'll tell you already. My pet peeve is POLITICAL CORRECTNESS.

Have you ever heard of such a dumb idea in your LIFE? I mean really. Make us learn ridiculous phrases for absolutely no reason.

Take the word "retarded". You can't say that anymore. Nope. Not allowed. Now they are "Mentally Challenged." THIS is not insulting.

HUH?

I mean it MEANS the same thing doesn't it? Look up retarded in the dictionary, it's not a cuss word. It's MEAN because PEOPLE made it MEAN. Does anyone SERIOUSLY think that Mentally Challenged doesn't get used the same way? It just doesn't roll off the tongue as easily, but cruel people will make the effort I assure you.

Prattle On - Teri Stricker

Garbage man. You remember him? He died. Now the same guy, doing the same thing, is a SANITATION ENGINEER. Uh huh. What is he engineering? Yeah, I don't know either. There is nothing at all wrong with being a garbage man. It's an important job. It's a smelly job, I grant you, also why it is so important. He takes all that smelly stuff away from our HOUSE. This is a good thing. So now he's a SANITATION ENGINEER. Whoopdie doo. Did this make his job any easier? Did a single duty change? No. Just words.

Maybe the first week it made said garbage man feel more, I don't know engineery. But, really NOTHING changed. And what the hell was wrong with garbage man? I don't recall being teased in the schoolyard with "you're a big fat garbage man!" My children didn't mention that particular epithet either.

NATIVE AMERICAN. Okay I understand they aren't Indians, but they aren't NATIVE either. They came here from somewhere else too. "Indians" came about because Columbus didn't know where he was, and it stuck. Okay I GET that. But Native Americans is no more correct. We don't know WHERE they came from. Australia called the folks that were already there aborigines, which was at least correct. They didn't originate there. Of course, everyone in Australia and America could call themselves the same. It's just as true.

So since neither term is right, why change it? It's to irritate us. Don't tell me about how Indian is an epithet. It's not. They don't like the images created by westerns. Changing the tag, does not change the image. Sorry. It doesn't. PEOPLE change images, not words. Meet some actual people of that culture, relate to them, those images die a quick death.

Lastly. It abbreviates to NA. That's always been "Not Applicable". It could get confusing, don't you think? Although I suppose putting Not Applicable in a Race blank would be kinda, doofy.

Some terms ARE bad. Like the "N" word. I don't like that word. Mean people were the only ones I ever heard use it.

Prattle On - Teri Stricker

The thing is none of the other tags work there either. It's not BLACK the skin is more a brown shade isn't it? For those fond of "Negro".. um.. that means black. So now they are African Americans. Other than being long, (I am lazy) it's descriptive. But you know what's going to happen? You KNOW we like to abbreviate. So now they're going to be AA's. Um .. back to not good now since AA has always been Alcoholic's Anonymous. On this one I don't know the answer. Dang .. I really wanted to know too.

Except - how come we can't just all be people? ESPECIALLY in the good old USA. My ancestors hailed from England, and Ireland, and the Netherlands, and who knows where else, and by the time you get down to me, I'm just an American. Heinz 57 all the way. Is that a bad thing? My family melted in the big melting pot. You can't chase all the trees down in your family as a rule, so you know, we could ALL have a little of everything in us. Think about THAT next time you want to be Racist. In fact, if you believe the Bible, we all came from the same place. Shoot, even if you go for the big bang thing, we originated in the same cell, didn't we? So knock the shit off, will ya?

Otherwise, why does that need to be on a form ANYWAY? We are not allowed to hire, rent, or anything else based on this information. So WHY ARE YOU ASKING?

Race might be an issue for medical things. Some of us get things more often than other races.

LITTLE PEOPLE. Okay I understand not liking "midget". But this one makes me think of leprechauns. Now, they are cute, leprechauns, but who wants to be seen in that light? I think it's way worse than midget. How do you get taken seriously when someone is thinking of little men with green outfits and top hats and selling Lucky Charms? I don't know. I just wouldn't like it, myself. At least little people is admitting they are people, and not bowling balls or something. And I'm glad they didn't decide (whoever came up with these PC terms to begin with I mean) on "height challenged". That would just suck.

Prattle On - Teri Stricker

You know, this chapter is gonna get me in trouble. But if I start shutting up NOW, then what's the point of the book? It's all about what I think. It ain't necessarily bout what's right for everyone.

The thing is, changing the words ain't the answer. You have to change PEOPLE. This really reminds me of the book, 1984. No, really. They believed that changing the WORDS would change how people thought. It didn't work, if you recall, Winston was a rebel, all the same. He got over the rebellion only by being tortured and brainwashed.

I can tell you the answer in one word. RESPECT. It's gone, and I don't know where the hell it went. Think of any crime in the universe as we know it, it boils down to lack of respect. Lack of respect for law, property, others, or self, it's still respect. Less respect, more crime. It's simple.

There, see? I solved the whole mystery. The only problem is I've not a clue how to fix it. People don't care about anything anymore. There's the almighty dollar, and there's STUFF. That they care about. Oh and ME. We're quite fond of ourselves.

I like ME too, I do. I just happen to think that YOU are pretty cool too. That's why I don't throw my garbage out the window of my car into your yard. That's why I treat people I meet with respect, and why I try to actually listen when people speak.

Lots don't. Go thru 10 lines at the supermarket. The checkout person always asks how you are. See how many people hear your answer. It's sad, but true. My son always says "horrible" or "rotten". You'd be surprised how many people say "that's nice". They don't listen, and they don't care.

Granted, I'm testing tired people who hate their jobs. That could be a factor, but you know, try it anywhere. See if I'm right..

So how to make people care? I don't know darn it. I make people laugh, they like that. I sing to them, they like that. But can I make them care? Probably not.

This chapter has a lesson in it. Don't write about pet peeves they aren't funny. But I'm glad I got it off my chest. I wonder does that mean I have to get new bras? I hope not, I'm not exactly well endowed to begin with.

So I step down from the orange crate soapbox thingy, turn off the overpoweringly loud microphone, and chapter. I bet you're ready to chapter. I don't blame you. But you're still here. WOW. I love you for that!

Ready set go and stuff.

Chapter Nine – The Bathroom

Now after making you listen to me rant for a whole chapter, I'm thinking that I should probably lighten up. Yep. I mean you're reading this in the bathroom, most likely, and stress isn't a good thing in the bathroom, so I hear.

I read in the bathtub. I get wrinkly, it's true. But it's warm, it's comfy, and there's no TV in there. DAD, he wants we should have a TV in there, but I'm not real fond of the idea.

You know in a family, the bathroom is the quiet place. It's the one place you are USUALLY guaranteed some privacy. Some families that's not so true, but in mine it always was.

So you can strip down and see, yes my ass really IS that big. But mostly, you can take a deep breath and say "Hi there Me. How the hell are you anyway?"

The bathroom is not always free of irritations. Like DAD rarely rinses the sink when he shaves. So you go to get a glass of water or wash your hands, and now you gotta clean that stuff up. If you're me, you growl a little doing it on those bad days.

Then there's the toilet paper problem. You just got home from well, somewhere, and you really HAVE to go. So you race for the bathroom, you slam the door behind you and you do your thing. Now you reach for the toilet paper.

Gone. Some sweet family member has used the last of it, and all that is left is that darling brown piece of cardboard. If that bathroom doesn't have a place for toilet paper, you are now trapped on the toilet.

So you yell out "Honey? Could you bring me some toilet paper?"

Crickets.

Great. So you read a few more pages of the bathroom book and you yell out again

"Honey?"

Prattle On - Teri Stricker

"WHAT!"

He's in a mood, now isn't he? Well we still have to ask, don't we? Because, well, we are TRAPPED. On the Toilet. And now your legs are going to sleep.

"I need toilet paper!" you call out as sweetly as you can manage.

"I'm in the other bathroom, you gotta wait!"

That explains the mood. He doesn't like talking when he's in the bathroom. I don't either. We match real well that way.

So by the time you get toilet paper, you can't feel your legs. You are maybe wondering if you will be paralyzed for life. But eventually you can hobble on out of there.

Now home alone is worse. Now you have to stand up and hobble out, pants at ankles, to the place we keep this stuff. YUK. So you see, families are good for something. They also give you people to blame for not replacing the toilet paper roll.

It really sucks when you're the one who forgot. I mean there's NO ONE to yell at. You can yell at yourself, but that is never as satisfying is it?

Then there are the bathroom mysteries. Like how does a 5 year old child manage to splash toothpaste at the top of a 4 foot mirror where the bottom is at the sink level? How do they DO that? It defies physics, I'm telling you. But my granddaughter can do it. She's a champion.

Then there's the pile of wet towels. Right beside the hamper. I've never understood that. Drop it two inches to the right and it is in the hamper. But they can't DO that.

And puddles. I hate puddles. My Son in Law is a champion puddle maker. He claims he doesn't NEED a towel. He's part Native American and so he dries fast he says.

HUH?

The puddles tell me a different story, ok?

Prattle On - Teri Stricker

I guess this is the bathroom chapter. I don't know quite why we need a bathroom chapter, but as we are now two pages in, I guess we are in the bathroom for a while.

Then there's the toothpaste. Takes, like what, a SECOND to put the cap back on the toothpaste? Kids cannot do this. I think it's a developmental problem. Their cap back on organ doesn't work or something. I don't know. And soon, the cap is lost. Gone. Kaput. Another mystery. Where do they go?

Kids ALSO have a defective "throw that away" organ, so obviously it didn't make it to the garbage. There's no room for it to go down the drain. So it's not there either. You search the floor with a magnifying glass. Nothing. Does it go to unused toothpaste cap heaven? I don't know, but it is NOT in the bathroom from whence it came.

Then there are the soap slivers. Multiple colors. Very pretty. We don't throw them away. I don't know why. We don't use them either. So here's this little melted soap design in the soap dish. Pink, blue, white. Lovely. At least until Mom gets crazy and cleans everything in sight, including the soap dish.

We don't have a guest towel. I refuse. No one will use it, what is the point? Everyone I know, there's the guest towel. Pristine. Who would dare touch it? Not this girl. Nope. So we don't have any. I refuse to buy things I won't use. I suppose you could think of it as an ornament, but with six people using the bathroom, no room for ornaments.

And did you ever notice that there is some shampoo you can't use? You bought it, it's in the bottle, and you can't get it out. So you sit it upside down so that NEXT time you can use the last of that shampoo. But it falls over somewhere in between your showers or baths and so there's 4 bottles of almost gone shampoo that you are BY GOD going to use someday.

Now before we leave the bathroom, that mysterious haven, I must go back to the toilet again. No I don't have to go, I didn't mean LITERALLY.

Prattle On - Teri Stricker

The female pet peeve is the toilet seat being left up. This does not bother me. Personally, I think we can look before we sit, we do have eyes, after all. But could you try HITTING the toilet? I mean really.

I mean, guys, I know you can aim. I have two children. I'm not St. Mary, I got them the usual way. This thing is not THAT big and the toilet bowl is HUGE in comparison, so tell me, please, what is the problem?

Why do we have to clean YUK off the rim, the sides of the toilet? This is bad, guys BAD. You should really be house-trained by now, you know?

My son, he tried to explain this whole "splash factor" thing. BZZZZZZZZT wrong answer. Get closer. It wasn't designed to be done from the other side of the room after all. Sigh. Well at least most of you don't pee in the corner. Or on my fence.

And while you are at it, rinsing the sink after shaving is not a bad thing. It's not hard. Really. I just don't see why I have to do it. I shave my legs, no one knows I did it. I rinse the tub. Voila. No hair in the tub. See? Like magic. Try it. You'll be amazed!

Prattle On - Teri Stricker
Chapter Ten – More Family

Well well. Chapter Ten. Can you believe it? This Jon, my online friend - Well one of them, I don't want you should think we have some hot thing going on. Anyway, this idea of his ain't so bad, I guess, since I'm still typing.

So, more family stuff. Family is what we are made of after all. GIRL, SLSIL, (remember? Silly Little Son In Law), MOM, DAD, GRANDGIRL AND GRANDBOY, we've all lived together a long time.

It's how families always were in the olden days. The nuclear family is rather new, historically speaking. WOW. That sounded smart. I should write that down. Wait, I just did. Okay, so much for smart. Let us move on, shall we?

So the first house we all lived in, along with BOY was a 3 bedroom ranch. No I'm not kidding, we didn't plan all this, it just, you know, happened. Although no grandkids then. GIRL and SLSIL had just married and GRANDGIRL was waiting to burst out upon us all.

So we talk to the landlord who we find has gotten a house from hell two doors down. But it is a HUGE house from hell. 5 bedrooms. SLSIL is good at carpentry, he claimed, and the drywall and all, we can all do together. (by the way he actually was good at carpentry).

So we go down to look. The picture window is a big board. You go in. Motorcycle tracks on the kitchen linoleum. Okay. This is interesting.

The living room carpet is bad, holes everywhere in the walls, but there is potential. He wants we should move in fast, because the kids in the area seem to have been "playing" here.

GIRL stays home. She don't like it, but as she is ready to drop GRANDGIRL she don't have much choice. We roll up our sleeves and get to work. Landlord and his son are doing the roof, replacing the kitchen floor, that stuff.

Prattle On - Teri Stricker

So cleaning and cleaning and some more cleaning first of all. The floor under the moldy carpet and all is cement, so this ain't so bad. No rotting wood to deal with.

Now, I'm not going to take you through the whole process, that would be boring, but upstairs in the master bedroom there is this, I don't know what. Cubby? Crooked closet? I don't know. I DO know I had to suit up for THAT. Used, um, condoms and other rot in there. I see how the kids PLAYED.

So we get to the point where the upstairs is livable. The downstairs is dusty from drywall dust and we are about to paint but GIRL can stay the hell upstairs while we do that. So we move in up there.

At the end of all the work we had a pretty nice looking place, shining white walls. So, we start our first winter.

Now, someone who is maybe not so smart, had put in a PVC pipe to the outside faucet. I don't know if you know this, but if PVC freezes, it shatters. So, not the greatest idea. Anyway a piece did shatter.

So SLSIL, he starts trying to take it out so we can replace it. SNAP! Here I must mention that I've done some plumbing in most of the houses we've lived in before we met and then wound up adding SLSIL to the family.

So he gets the whole assembly out and we decide we need to replace this with galvanized. So I say I'll take BOY's GIRLfriend and go get it.

No way. You'll get the wrong stuff and we'll have to go return it all anyway. So I tell him I was fixing this crap before he was born and was perfectly capable of picking up some pipe.

So he goes to DAD. DAD, I guess, is supposed to stop me from this horrendous thing I am planning to do. DAD laughs so hard he nearly falls out of his chair, and tells him exactly the same thing I did.

Now he goes to BOY. Why he would think BOY could possibly stop MOM, I know not. Perhaps he just wanted to vent. So he tells BOY all about it.

BOY promptly laughs himself silly, and says the same thing as the rest of us.

SLSIL gives up. He figures he's going to come home from work and have to return everything, and do it all himself.

So, me and GIRLfriend go to the local hardware store, I take the assembly with me. I go to the counter, show my lovely pipe system and say, "I need this in galvanized"

"Come back in 30 minutes"

Done. I may have paid less at Home Depot or something, it's true. But it was much less work, and closer to the house.

SLSIL comes home looks at it, says it won't fit.

UH HUH. Humor the old woman, try it. Like a glove. Of course. This is not brain surgery.

This was maybe SLSIL's first glimpse that MOM wasn't quite the helpless flower. I don't know for sure, mind reading is not one of my talents.

Now, I have a cat. He was a stray, I think someone dropped him off in the country where we lived, and so he showed up at our house. Anyway, this was before the SLSIL came into our lives when GIRL was still our little girl, subject to our rules, you know yada yada. The FAMILY named him Top Cat, yes, after the cartoon. By the end of the day he was just TC.

TC is a Maine Coon. Long hair. Lazy. At the time very skinny. Not so much now. So when we moved to the new house, so did TC.

This house had been empty a while so there are mice. TC doesn't kill mice. That is too much like work. He scared one to death, that's about it.

So how to get rid of the mice. These mice, they take the food from the traps without springing them. I think maybe they are very smart mice. Maybe related to Speedy Gonzales.

Prattle On - Teri Stricker

By the time we moved, there were less mice, but still mice. Here and there one runs over your foot in the dark. You jump. Then you go on.

So, SLSIL finds this great house, great price, reasonable neighborhood. By now we have both GRANDGIRL and GRANDBOY.

So new house. We clean some carpets, that's about all it needed. Rather nice change from the last place. About two months in, TC has decided he is the great white hunter after all, and catches a mouse. Of course, since he's not REALLY the great white hunter, he doesn't kill it.

The thing is, he brings it INTO this gorgeous house. SLSIL hits the roof. He is moving things, running around trying to catch this mouse. I don't know any mouse that would not have been embarrassed by being caught if he'd been caught that night. The whole time he is screaming "There is a MOUSE in my HOUSE!"

I have to tell you I was just DYING of laughter. I mean not only is he after this mouse in the worst possible way, but he's RHYMING on top of it. I was not sure I was going to survive that night.

Anyway, once he calmed down, naturally being not an idiot, he knew there was no catching that mouse that night. Meanwhile they have gotten a cat since we moved in. Oscar. The next day Oscar chases the mouse. He didn't even TRY to actually catch it.

Day three. Now SLSIL is still quite upset. He doesn't want this mouse gnawing in the walls and all, and the cats are useless. I am in my office doing my little officy things, and I hear GIRL yell;

"OH MY GOD!!!!"

I am thinking a grandchild is bleeding. So I run up the steps to the kitchen where the ruckus is going on.

GRANDBOY, who is maybe two years old at this time, has chased this mouse into a plastic glass. GIRL is losing her mind. She is not running in circles, but it is obvious she doesn't know what to do. So I grab a kitchen towel, cover the top of the cup with it and pick it up.

By this time I'm not sure it's even in there anymore, but I go outside with covered cup, and dump it. Out runs the mouse into the back yard. Mouse is no longer in the house, and my two year old grandson is a hero.

I tell you, I couldn't make this stuff up.

Tell me life isn't funny. Go on, I DARE you.

Yeah I know, wow, it's time to chapter. Where DOES the time go?

Chapter Eleven - Pets

So you've met the family. And survived. This is a good thing, not everyone does. I kid. There are no dead visitors in my yard. Or the river for that matter. I told you, I am harmless.

We've had a few pets over the years. I've had an orange Tabby who DAD thought was a girl and we named Kiara. I liked the name. GIRL is lucky she didn't get it. Anyway, Kiara was not a girl, we learned when we took him to get fixed. So he was Kitty ever after.

Kitty we got as a kitten. The kids adored Kitty, and Kitty mostly liked them. He was de-clawed in the front paws so as to save the furniture, but we left the back in case he ever got out.

I had to teach the children he was not a toy, of course. This is normal I suppose. No, leave his tail alone, no his front paws are NOT handles do not drag him like that.

Kitty was a killer. Anything smaller than him was food. So we got a gerbil.

Buddy.

BOY loved Buddy, he was, well, his Buddy. I was maybe a bit overprotective of Buddy, but you know, we had killer Kitty to worry about.

So we had Buddy nearly 3 years. He got out once. He camped out in the laundry room under the washer and / or dryer. I tried everything to catch that damn gerbil. Sneak up and try to catch him, lure him with food... he'd come out, but run like hell when he saw me.

BOY comes home from school. Looks in cage.

"Where's Buddy?"

"Back here, refusing to be caught." I say.

BOY brings the tank out. Lays it on its side. Puts the food in there. Ten minutes later Buddy is in the cage, cage jerked upright, home at last.

Dang kid. Why didn't I think of that?

Then came the parakeets. First one we had maybe six months. He learned how to open the cage while we were on a family outing. Kitty ate him.

Second one, he got out in the middle of the night, ran into a door, we thought. There are no signs that Kitty got him. A fact Kitty seems kind of upset about.

So for the third one, we get a better cage.

Beautiful little bird. Sweet. Sammy. He's in his cage, he hasn't learned to go out of his cage, and HIS wings are clipped so he can't fly out anyway, only climb his cage. Safe.

Wrong. I come home from the neighbors. He's in the cage. Toes up.

Not a sniffle did this bird have. So I call the gas company open all doors and windows.

They find a leak. "Not enough to kill a bird though"

I said "Go look in that cage over there. It was enough" So Sammy maybe saved our lives, I don't know.

Then came Georgie. Georgie was green and a barrel of laughs. He would dive bomb Kitty. We got him at Walmart. I just picked the bird that irritated the crap out of all the other birds, and I brought him home.

For two weeks I didn't let him out of the cage. We'd talk to him and try and get him to sit on our finger. The kids and I said "It's okay" in a soothing voice a lot.

Georgie turned out quite friendly, and talked. First he said "It's okay" in that same soothing tone.

GIRL liked to sneak out and look at the TV when she was supposed to be doing dishes. So DAD or I would say "Get back in the kitchen!" That was Georgie's second phrase.

Georgie lived through two houses. He lived through a three day power outage. He lived thru BOY giving him a bath with soap.

That was my fault. BOY was cleaning the cage. At the same time Georgie is taking a bath under the sprayer. DAD and I were on our way out the door to a customer. I said "Use Soap"

He thought I meant the bird. Dish soap no less. So for three days we had Georgie in the bathroom, the warmest room in the house. Rinsing that poor bird over and over again.

He made it. He was even friendlier after that, since we handled and cuddled him so much through all that.

Then a year later he got a cold for no reason. By the time they show you they don't feel good, it's over. Broke my heart. MOM was done with birds.

Now we all know there are strays. But we found a stray RABBIT. No, I'm not kidding. He was a Himalayan something or other, hanging out in our yard.

BOY goes outside; rabbit does not run off like other rabbits. He keeps his distance, but no running. So BOY gets some cat food, goes back out. Rabbit comes right up and eats it, then allows BOY to pick him up.

Now we have to buy a cage and all for Rabbit. Oh joy. But kids are only kids once you know. When the kids stopped paying enough attention to him, I put him in the paper and another family took him to love him some more.

I had two hamsters as well. The first one was cute enough. And social enough once you cornered him and got him out of the cage. Pet store hamster. He got sick, he died, have no idea why.

The second one the grandkids named Nemo. I wasn't looking for a hamster. I always go look at the pets at Walmart, whether I've any kids with me or not. She was a golden hamster and she WANTED to go home with me. She came right up to the glass and visited. I walked away she followed me to the corner of the tank and looked so darned forlorn I had to get her.

I didn't have to chase Nemo. I'd open the door, cup my hands, she'd walk right out. She was a real charmer. She learned how to open the door herself. She'd get out. The first time I thought Oh my dear we are never going to find her. So I'm looking, this is in my office, and the door was wide open when she got out, so I'm thinking she ran right out that door. But I better look anyway.

There she is. Right at my chair. Cup my hands there she is. I still didn't know how she got out.

Next night I'm singing, headphones on. Something furry on my foot. It's Nemo. Nemo is not stupid. She won't try when I am watching.

So MOM gets sneaky and turns on the webcam. Zoom in on cage door. Go back to singing but, watch the cam.

She would hang from the top of the cage wall and KICK the door open. So I found a paperclip to secure the door. Voila. I miss Nemo. I left her with BOY when I moved to Tennessee. I didn't think she would like the long trip. TC came along, was even better on the trip than I expected him to be.

You know what? It's already time to chapter. I think TC will be my only pet for a while. I enjoyed the zoo and all as the kids grew up, but they are work after all.

So let us Chapter and be done with it, what do you say?

Prattle On - Teri Stricker
Chapter Twelve – Commercials Suck

Sooner or later I have to shut up. Right? I mean you would think I'd run out of stupid things to tell you about. But then there are still subjects we haven't touched on yet.

Like commercials. Those irritating things between the programs. Some nights I think there are more minutes of commercials than programs. However you need them sometimes to make a bathroom run. Or to make the popcorn.

You got your Coca Cola commercials, you got the Pepsi, you got the antacids, you got it all. Then there's the embarrassing ones.

You know the ones I'm talking about. You are 16 watching TV with your boyfriend, and up comes.

Woman and younger woman walking in a field of lovely flowers. They have this Vaseline on the camera lens romantic blur thing going on. Chintzy music in the background and the younger woman says.

"Mom, you ever have that "not so fresh feeling?"

Right. My mom and me, we always walked through fields of flowers and talking about douching. NOT.

I can picture that conversation. My mother was no nonsense. She had nothing against flowers but, we'd have had to drive a little to find said field. Anyway, I can picture it.

"Mom, you ever had that "not so fresh feeling?"

First that LOOK. You know the one. The raised eyebrow, the disbelieving almost smile. Yeah, that one. Then she'd have said. "For Christ's sake Teri take a damn BATH!"

Then there's the oh so wonderful sanitary napkin commercials. These are necessary products, but you know, I just don't need that kind of information while I'm eating dinner.

"Always with WINGS". What? I want my pads to FLY now? I think not.

Prattle On - Teri Stricker

My husband is a real man. He can handle going to the store for my womanly products. He can hold my purse while I go to the fitting room. He can carry my bags when we're shopping. What more could a woman want?

You always know the newly married men. Those are the ones that are holding the purse, their eyes darting around because they hope no one sees.

Or at the store buying those womanly needs. He buys all kinds of stuff he doesn't need then kind of sneaks the womanly thing in the midst of it all. What? He thinks maybe the clerk has never seen a man purchase these things? His wife is the only woman who ever sent her man to the store?

I digressed again, didn't I? Well like I said, this whole book is one long digression, you should be used to this by now.

DAD, he tells me I have a mind like a steel sieve. He's right, you know. So back to commercials.

I grant you there are some great ones, some funny ones, that actually MEAN to be funny. But you know, they are still irritating when you want to know what happens next on Boston Legal.

Then there's the ever popular infomercial. I know because I wake up to them. DAD he's not so good at turning off the TV before he goes to sleep. They are usually on at 3AM. How to become a millionaire. Of course, they don't actually tell you how to do that, they spend their half hour convincing you why you should buy their course on how to become a millionaire. I've watched a few minutes of a few out of mild curiosity. They have the same chintzy music as the douche commercial in some cases.

None of us are good enough, are we? We're too fat, too skinny, too tall, too short. We have lines, and wrinkles, we have hair in embarrassing places, and hair that doesn't shine or glow, or whatever it is supposed to do.

So we need this diet, this make up, this hair remover, this this this. You do NOT. Good Lord get a GRIP already. I mean, we are human beings and stuff. You get older you are SUPPOSED to get crows feet and lines in your face. You EARNED them.

I do wear makeup on occasion, I even color my hair from time to time. It's not BAD. But if it is this all important THING, you really need to lighten up. I know women who won't leave the house without paint all over their face. The hair has to be just so. And on and on and on. Plucking the eyebrows. OW! No, I'm not doing that, thanks so much for asking.

You are just going to have to look at my manly eyebrows and deal with it. Oh if they start growing together I may pluck the middle, but those archy things, no, I'll pass.

It's just that, you know I'm me. Slather my face with paint, pluck me, liposuction me, if I'm not happy with me, none of that is going to help. No matter what I do I am not going to look like, say Shania Twain, who doesn't even look like Shania Twain.

Really. I don't know WHAT she looks like but no one's face is that perfect. That's 4 layers of powder there. Same with Martina McBride, and Dolly Parton, and anyone else who has to be out there under the lights and cameras. Under all that makeup kids, it's just another person. With lines, and imperfections.

See? I'm sneaking in some wisdom and hoping you don't notice.

When I slather on the makeup I do it right, the foundation the powder, all that crap. But most of the time my face is naked. Is it supreme confidence, indifference, or laziness? I don't know, but so far I don't scare small children in Walmart, so I think I'm ok

So commercials suck. See, back on topic. Actually, we never left. Those commercials leave you feeling like you need all their stuff to make you worthy or something. Or that's their goal anyway.

We are smarter than that, I hope.

Men, don't you laugh you are no better. You don't go get your hair cut anymore, you get it STYLED. Some men spend more time with their hair these days than I do.

And clothing my goodness we've created male clotheshorses. Just look at you. In your Calvin Klein underwear and your designer jeans. And what is that "sorta unshaven" thing all about? Why is that sexy to the young women?

To me it looks like maybe you should go home and shave. But I'm old. Either shave or don't shave.

And what MASOCHIST came up with the whole leg shaving thing? I shave my legs, now for days they itch. Maddeningly. When it stops. Guess what? Time to shave again. It dries out the skin, you get ingrown hairs, it SUCKS. Whoever you are that came up with this torture, I am NOT your friend.

I tell you there are times I want to go live in a cave and just go hairy.

Then there is SPANDEX. What IS Spandex? I think it's something to induce vomiting. Maybe these young perfect shaped girls can get away with it, but for the rest of us it just doesn't work. The cellulite SHINES right through. Every little lump.

This would be no big deal, but so many who should not wear it, they don't KNOW they shouldn't wear it. I don't understand. If you are 5'4" and 200lbs, why do you not know that spandex is not for you?

High heels. Another sadistic thing. I have a cousin she says she is most comfortable in heels. HIGH heels. She's a little crazy this cousin. For the rest of us, this is a torture device. At least for those who wear them. I don't see the point of wearing heels to a job where you are on your feet all day long. This is not terribly smart. Your back is going to be gone in no time, I tell you.

For an office job, it's maybe not so bad, you walk to the bathroom and the coffee mess. I wear low heels myself.

Prattle On - Teri Stricker

Women also like shoes. I have nothing against shoes, they keep your feet warm. But Imelda Marcos I am not. I have white, I have brown, I have black. If an outfit won't go with any of the three, well I'm not buying it.

Maybe I'll buy a special outfit and matching shoes when I get my Pulitzer. Until then, we are not made of money and must deal with what we have.

I know women who can pull clothes out and make an outfit to die for. I'm not one of them. I pull out clothes and go, uh huh.

Accessories? What are they? I have one purse. It's black. It'll do.

I have a belt, it holds my pants up. I have a cowboy hat, and in a burst of inspiration, tied a scarf on it. That's it. That's my accessories.

I have jewelry. It's pretty. It never comes out of my jewelry box. I need jewelry to go to Walmart?

But I do okay. I leave the house people don't point and laugh. I get along with people. They don't notice the duct tape on my heel.

You know, we're just folks. There's absolutely nothing wrong with folks. If we all looked like Shania Twain, then what would be special? The men would get confused. The drool would flood the earth. Who needs it, I ask you?

So it's time to chapter. I'm really rambling now. I can't believe you're still here. I mean you have to be at least as nutty as me. I don't know if I'd read this crap, myself. Wait, yes I would. I read cereal boxes for pity's sake.

So Chapter already.

Prattle On - Teri Stricker
Chapter Thirteen – Superstition & Stuff

Thirteen. It's a good thing I'm not superstitious, this is all I'm saying. If YOU are, well, just pretend this is twelve again, and you'll be okay. I mean you're reading a book, not climbing a mountain, right? What could go wrong?

OW. I just fell out of my chair. Leaned just a little too far back, I guess.

So I guess superstition might be a good topic, what do you think? Do you quake with fear on Friday the Thirteenth? I don't. Just another day. I have bad days, I have clumsy days, they just don't fall on the thirteenth, that's all.

That movie came out when I was fifteen. I went to the drive in with my boyfriend. We watched the movie. You know, I should have known he'd turn out to be gay.

Anyway that was back when those kind of movies got me. Now, not so much. I've gotten jaded. But that night I was fifteen and the boyfriend had to walk me to the bathroom and back.

My best friend had a black cat. Snoopy. Ok, I don't know why a black cat was named Snoopy. It just WAS, okay? But Snoopy crossed my path a lot. I lived.

She also crossed our board games a lot. Clue, Parcheesi, Chinese checkers, she really wasn't fussy. Oh, I didn't mention the black cat named Snoopy was a she? Sorry. She was a she. Kittens all the time. Everywhere.

Now, walking under a ladder, I haven't tried that. It's not that it worries me I just don't run into a lot of walk underable ladders. Usually if there's a ladder, I am holding it so my husband doesn't fall off of it.

If I let go and walk under it, he maybe falls. But that would be HIS bad luck wouldn't it?

Prattle On - Teri Stricker

The salt thing. What is that? Spill salt so you toss some over a shoulder. Interesting concept. Never tried it. My son, he spilled the whole carton on the counter when he was 3. He had no more bad luck than if it had been sugar. I mean the bad luck was actually spilling it in the first place, don't you think?

A rabbit's foot brings good luck. Never tried that. Doesn't sound terribly lucky for the rabbit either way.

Step on a crack, break your mother's back. I remember this one. I tortured myself like a month trying to miss cracks. But after that month, I stepped on them a lot. My mother had many problems, but her back, it was fine.

Garlic protects from evil spirits and vampires. I adore garlic, I eat a lot of it. Coincidently, I've run into no bad spirits or vampires. You know, they might have something here.

An itchy palm means money will come your way. You know I heard it had to be the RIGHT palm. I've been robbed. My left one itched a LOT. Never got a dime. Dang.

It is bad luck to sleep on a table. Okay, yeah, it is bound to hurt your back. Who the hell sleeps on tables anyway?

To make a happy marriage, the bride must wear: something old, something new, something borrowed, something blue. You know, I had all that. But so did all the women that got divorced within 5 years. So I'm thinking, sweet custom, but it don't hold water.

Warm hands, cold heart; This one is definitely a crock. My husband, he's a walking heater. I kid you not. I will never need an electric blanket. He steams up the windows of the car when it's cold outside. He has the warmest heart you ever saw. Cries at sad movies. So nope, another one bites the dust.

So you know, superstitions, they don't work so good. Maybe I am just ridiculously lucky and so have missed all these things.

What? You walked under a ladder and a bucket of paint hit you in the head? That's just awful. Tell you what, we will chapter and you can read fourteen in the emergency room.

You should put a wet cloth on that it doesn't look so good.

Chapter Fourteen – No Idea

Feel better? You know, it could have been worse. Thirteen stitches, but it didn't crack your skull or addle your brains. You can still read this crap.

So we've survived the big thirteen. That's an accomplishment. We've cruised through so many pages of my drivel, it's unreal. You'd think I'd run out of drivel. I mean really. Even I didn't know I had this much drivel in me. Evidently I've stored it up over the years.

I was a tomboy. You might have guessed. I caught frogs and snakes. I played baseball, not that I was good at it. I played football until the guys started tackling us whether we actually had the football or not. I climbed trees, all that stuff.

I never really outgrew it. Oh I'm 45 years old, I don't climb trees anymore, but neither does DAD. I don't think BOY does anymore either, come to think of it. That squirrel incident might have traumatized him you know.

But I'm not real girly. You know painting all the toes and fingers and all. Once in a while GIRL and I would do the hair thing, and the makeup thing, and it was fun, but not really my thing.

I taught my son the mighty art of frog catching. I was really a terrible mother. He'd bring in a snake, and I'd go "COOL! Let's see if we can look up what kind that is!"

It must have been awful. He comes in, waving the snake waiting for my screams. Ah well, we can't all be perfect, can we.

For his elementary years, we lived down the street from the beach. It was a private beach for those on that road. So we swam, we fished, we caught turtles, it was all good.

Prattle On - Teri Stricker

I once caught two fish at the same time. Well for a minute. I fish for the little guys. Sunfish, Blue Gills. So I'm watching my bobber and sitting on the dock. Well I decided it was time to reel it in and find another spot to bobber watch. I reel it in and suddenly a bass hits. Get him nearly out of the water and he lets go.. of a little sunfish who never made my bobber go down. My son and husband couldn't believe it, and they saw it. We tell that story a lot. So it goes here.

When I was a kid, I liked pretty rocks. You know, sparkly. My son, he liked rocks too, but he wanted a rock BOOK, and he had to know what they were. These were interesting expeditions, we both learned things.

There were interesting accidents with BOY. He never had normal ones. At two he put his finger in the wrong side of the screen door while GIRL opened it and needed stitches.

He lost a divot of flesh out of his head playing with golf clubs in the house.

He ricocheted himself in the hand with a bb gun. This one needs a little explaining. He followed the rules. There was a milk carton and a stump. He wore the goggles he pointed the gun only where he meant to shoot. He did it all right.

He missed the carton, hit the stump, bb ricocheted right into the web of his hand. No yell loud enough to hear.

So he came into the house. TOLD me he shot himself in the hand and went into the bathroom. It took a full minute for me to realize what he said. I kid you not. It like went in one ear, out the other, then sorta eased back.

So he's cleaning his wound and I said "You did WHAT?"

He STILL thinks this is hilarious. That's my BOY. So, after he's been sitting there a while messing, I realize the bb is still in his hand. He didn't quite mention that. I let him try a little to get it out. DAD wasn't home with the car, and there was really no way to stop him anyway.

Prattle On - Teri Stricker

So once DAD got home we went and got that bb out. BOY claims to this day he could have gotten it out. Perhaps he could have. I preferred the doctor.

The memory he likes best is our birthday walk. It was my birthday. I forget exactly which one. I want to say 35, but who knows. We took a walk in the woods behind the house. It's a nice day in March, mostly, if you are wearing a jacket. I have, as usual, my big 20 oz Wesco cup of coffee, and we're going about. For those not from where I am. Wesco is a gas station chain. Like Shell.

Well I was lost. I think I mentioned I'm not so good with directions, and unlike my son I don't know east from west. He was leading the way, and it wasn't that horrible. The woods isn't THAT big and it is surrounded by houses, so go straight long enough you are going to come out somewhere relatively soon.

We came to a little stream. There's a log across it. I go first. I crawl across the log, because I really don't trust my balance all that well, and that water is damn cold. Especially since we're lost. Oh BOY says he knows exactly where he is, but you know, he's going to be a man one day, and men NEVER admit they are lost.

So I get halfway across the log and I toss my coffee cup to the far bank. This struck BOY as supremely funny. To this day I don't know why. It was nearly empty, and I could crawl way better without it. Eventually we hiked our way home, had some hot cocoa and life was good.

Today as I type this with a fond smile, I'm 45. You know, it doesn't seem like it was TEN years ago. Time flies, doesn't it? The only time it doesn't is when you are waiting for something.

Birthdays are fun, but you know, age is just a number. Really. I can't run like I did at 10 years old, but the upside of that is, I don't want to run. Pretty much the only way to get me to run is to scare the crap out of me.

My son can tell you that's not the wisest course, scaring me. I whip around so fast you get smacked. THEN I figure out I am not going to die.

Prattle On - Teri Stricker

GIRL learned after many years to shut up when I hurt myself. She always asked too fast. Let me figure it out first. I slam my finger in the door like a moron and I'm deciding whether to scream or not, and hear.

"Wow MOM are you ok?"

"NO! I'm dying now shut up and let me die in PEACE already!"

So, better to wait a minute. THEN ask.

I'm also odd about getting hurt. I put a nail through my foot by stepping on a board I shouldn't have been stepping on.

All the way to the house I am cussing. "Stupid Stupid STUPID!" quietly. My teenaged son is following behind. So he says "That's where I get it!"

"What?"

"Calling myself names when I get hurt."

"Sure blame me. I can take it"

I was taught to be brave. No screaming and carrying on, you see. My babies were born with some groaning, but no screaming. I had a nurse tell me I was the quietest woman she ever assisted with. I don't believe this, but I'll take it, what the heck.

It wasn't all roses. With the first I got mad. Spitting mad. I'd read every book ever written about childbirth. I was ready for the labor. I was READY. I knew the contraction thing, I knew that the back could hurt. Not one of them mentioned the legs. My legs hurt and I was pissed.

The nurse was really big and adjusting things, but she was also GOOD. I missed her every time. Finally I spat out. "WHY do my LEGS hurt?"

Transition is a bitch, ain't it? So she goes and asks the doctor.

Turns out it was just because I'm a little woman. All that pressure had to go somewhere. So to the legs it went.

For some reason that was enough. To know why. I quit cussing and carrying on and went on from there.

Now, before you think I'm some birth giving HERO, I must tell you, I had ridiculously easy births. My daughter was born in 4 hours. My son, labor MIGHT have edged on two hours maximum.

So brave. I think that goes with the tomboy thing, right? It better, I'm not moving it.

Time again to chapter. So much drivel, so little time. My foot's asleep. Yep. Time to chapter.

Prattle On – Teri Stricker
Chapter Fifteen – In The Navy

You know, this could get to be a habit, typing drivel. The question is whether this is a good habit, or a bad one. Well, I think it's probably better than going out and buying drugs. Less likely to land me in jail, at any rate. Drivel isn't against the law. Yet.

I was a child once. It's true. I was really very little like this driveling idiot you see today. I was going to be a nurse when I grew up. I was serious. Then I found out about blood. How there's usually a lot of it to clean up when you're a nurse. And bedpans. Bedpans didn't make me happy. So, I'm not a nurse.

I was a smart child. Straight A's I got for many years. I really don't know what happened after that. Life, or something. As I may have mentioned, I grew up in Michigan, in a small town.

As I was getting to that age of choosing colleges, I wasn't straight A's anymore, I was more B's and C's. I wasn't less smart, but I cared a lot less about the grades. I'd discovered boys. Yeah, I know, smooth move ex-lax. But I was a poor kid and didn't think college was in my future anyway.

My parents were both blue collar. Stood on their feet in factories all day long. Even worse, as I came of age, most of the factories were leaving Michigan. Or at least my corner of it.

So no award winning grades, small town, boring. Like every teenager on the planet I wasn't real fond of the whole having parents thing either. So I joined the Navy. I did the early graduation thing, so in February of 1981 I went to boot camp. I was 17, turned 18 in boot camp. No cake. It sucked.

Boot camp is a lot of pushups. Some running. You get yelled at, but you know, you're young, you're used to it.

After boot camp is technical training school. Mine was Naval Technical Training School, Cory Station. Those of us who have been there, we just call it Cory Junior High.

In this time period, a military ID card was a ticket to beer, booze, whatever you want. Back then they figured you can get shot at for your country, maybe you should have a beer. Now you get shot at without the beer.

Of course, I was in during peacetime. No bullets to dodge. I'm not real fast, so that was a good thing. Not that I was in a rating that would get me shot at anyway. I was a Cryptologic Technician, Operations. CTO for short. I tell you anything else, I have to kill you. Okay, maybe not, maybe I only have to maim you. Anyway, it was a job. I had to have a security clearance for it. I was 18, and full of myself, but no more than most.

I learned stuff at Cory. That's what we went there for. But a lot of the stuff I learned wasn't in the classroom. Like that guys want sex. All the time. You walk past a group of guys, that's all they seemed to talk about.

Your ass. Yep, I had one, it is helpful to sitting. Other than that I didn't know what all the hoorah was about.

Now, understand, I never found myself terribly attractive. There were a zillion women more attractive, so what they saw in MY ass, I don't know. I mean, it wasn't misshapen or anything but, it was just, you know, an ass. Sailors are kind of like construction workers.

So at Cory we drank, we flirted, hopefully we learned what they tried to teach us and then you get your first set of orders.

I'm sitting at my desk and they tell me I'm going to Terceira, Azores.

Ok. But where is that?

Turns out there's some dust off the coast of Portugal in the Atlantic. The dust you can't brush away off the map that's the Azores.

So I went over on a C3. You sit in a net. They call them MAC flights. I call them loud. There's no insulation. So it's not like flying good old American Airlines where there's just this hum. They give you earplugs, they're nice people. They make my ears itch.

Prattle On - Teri Stricker

So I'm sitting in a net for 9 hours or however long that flight was, and I have odd things about traveling. I can't sleep. Even on a normal plane, or in a car, can't do it. I also can't read. I read while traveling I get nauseous. So I sit there and look at the other people in the other nets.

Did I say it was loud? At first we tried the conversational tactic. But it's loud plus you got the ear plugs. So you yell. That gets old fast. So you go back to sitting and looking at each other.

Eventually, you get where you are going.

In the Navy when you transfer, you have a sponsor. This is some other person that knows the ropes and helps you out. It's a good program. So your sponsor meets you at the airport, takes you to the base, introduces you around, all that neat stuff. It mostly works.

The island is green. It is mild in climate. Not too hot, not to cold. Usually. The "natives" are Portuguese; the streets are cobblestone, and narrow, very narrow. These narrow streets are lined with rock walls, rocks piled just high enough to usually keep the livestock in. Speeding is not smart. You come wheeling around a corner you are likely to hit someone's donkey, and that someone is sure to not be happy about it. Neither will your car.

It's a beautiful place and very not American. It's another country. They are all foreigners over there. Well, we are the foreigners in this case, but you would be surprised how many Americans don't see it that way.

So here I was. I am 18. I am very far from home. It is November. The winds are high. Someone said 75-80 mph winds were normal in the autumn. I don't know I didn't measure, but I walked out of the barracks and landed flat on my ass. I still had my ass because the guys at Cory didn't get it.

So you learn a sort of stomp, to make your way in the wind. It's not very sexy, but your ass feels much better. They used to say I could open my coat and fly to the NCO Club. That's the Enlisted club. You dance, you drink, you play pool, same as any other bar, I guess.

Prattle On - Teri Stricker

The thing is, women were outnumbered 10 to 1 by men. This is an odd feeling. You walk into the club, and where you walk in is the restaurant part.

Every male head turns and looks at you. It's a very odd feeling. You check your zipper, check to see if your shirt is inside out. Nope. So what the hell are they looking at? I had no idea.

So you walk thru to the bar, and you order a drink. Military people become friends quickly. They come and they go, no matter where you are stationed, but some become your best friends for a while. I suppose College could be the same, I don't know, I didn't go to college.

As a woman, outnumbered as we were, men buy you drinks and give you a lot of attention. This can do things to the ego. You maybe start thinking you are the hottest woman on the planet. I wasn't a real confident person, so for me it was more like, maybe I'm not so ugly as I thought.

But for the girls who did decide they were God's gift to men, I really wondered what would happen when they got back to what we termed "the real world". Would they be crushed for life not to be the center of attention every time they left their room? I don't know, I never saw.

People in the military are the same as everywhere. We were just people. We were young. We were proud of our uniform, proud to be in the military. But it was a job, you know? On the island were also the Air Force, and this was actually a Portuguese Air Force base, so you see them in uniform as well.

So, I am a hot property, and I am rich. The US dollar was strong and the Portuguese one was not. I was single and hadn't opened a sears account or anything else. I lived in the barracks so no rent. We worked weird hours, so I got paid extra to eat. That's rich. Okay, I couldn't afford a mansion on the hill, but to tell the truth I've never pined for one. But I could save a couple weeks and buy my first stereo. I could buy clothes, be a tourist, drink all I wanted, eat anywhere I liked, it was nice. I've never been so rich before or since.

Prattle On - Teri Stricker

So I decided I wanted to see the island, besides the bars we all piled into someone's car to go to. I call a cab. I ask how much to just cruise around and stop to look at things when I want for a few hours. $20. Even then, this wasn't a lot of money. So very cool. He will even show me some of the most interesting places.

Very cool. So we go. He showed me some interesting caves and took me to a gorgeous park, things like this. He also mentioned that they were having the running of the bulls that day.

Like I said, they are Portuguese. The running of the bulls is very interesting. I ran with them. Just, not on purpose.

We get to where all this is going on, I buy the driver a beer and we climb up somewhere and sit on the wall. Standing in the street the top of the wall is about a foot over my head.

They let off a firecracker or something to tell you they are letting the bulls loose, or that the bulls are back in the pen.

So I watch a run, they run out of sight. After a while the firecracker goes off, the vendors roll their carts into the street, we go for a beer.

Suddenly people are running. This can't be good. I look. There are bulls running at me. I am not completely stupid. I run.

I'm young, I'm in the Navy, I'm not in rotten shape, but I'm also terrified. I wasn't exactly planning to be all daring and run with the bulls. I'm holding a plastic glass of beer and it's naturally spilling everywhere.

I guess my face showed all this because another runner stopped and hoisted me up on the wall. Gracias! MUCHAS Gracias!!! So that was my running with the bulls.

Worse, I'd spilled my beer. I never let go of the glass.

I am a bouncer backer, so once I was safe, the heart rate returned to normal, my face lost that look of terror, and I watched. Later the cab driver and I found each other and he took me home. Overall it was a good day, and gave me a story I've told over and over through the years.

I have fond memories of those days. I grew up there. I had my first devastating heartbreak there. I learned how to deal with men in general, sort of. And I got pregnant.

It's not what I meant to do or anything, but there I was. It's okay, it all turned out. I got wonderful daughter out of it, and stuff.

But you know, I've gotten ahead of myself. Again. I did warn you about the rambling thing. I'm pretty sure it's time to chapter though. We can't have this chapter getting out of hand and taking over the book after all.

Prattle On - Teri Stricker
Chapter Sixteen – Ah, Youth

Sweet Sixteen. Maybe. I don't know, we'll see how it turns out.

We are still wandering about the Azores. Rambling. I was like any 18 – 19 year old. I had morals, just not when they got in my way. I didn't sleep around, not a new guy every night or anything, I just wasn't the Virgin Mary either.

See, the thing is guys want sex, girls want love. So girls, we translate sex to love. It's NOT by the way. In case you wondered. It can be a PART of love, a fun part, but it's not love. However, you learn that with time, don't you?

So I had a boyfriend or two, and in between I was hit on like all the rest of the girls. At first you have no idea how to respond. Especially if you were not the High School Homecoming Queen or something. But it's okay, you learn.

The first few times, you just run like hell. Then you try just ignoring them. Neither works real well. The running, well, you just wind up getting hit on by someone ELSE, and you never get to finish the conversation. The ignoring works a LITTLE better, but not much. They think maybe you are deaf and move closer.

Now, keep in mind you are in a bar. No One, including yours truly, is completely sober. I didn't get drunk a lot. I got really really really drunk once. That was quite enough. This was shortly after I landed on the island.

I was at a table with a group of people, some of them guys. I'd been wandering about the base, playing tourist, so I had my camera stuff with me at the table. I have pictures. Sometimes I look at them

I remember that night. For a long time I wished I didn't. But you know, it's part of the growing up stuff, and so it don't bother me so much now. First I played pool and a guy near the table, he grabbed something he should not have.

I put down the pool stick turned around, and put him against the wall. Now, I may have mentioned, I'm not so big. I was 5'4" tall and 107lbs. I looked like a toothpick with a big ass. Anyway, I digress. Again.

So I have this guy against the wall, my hand is on his neck. Obviously, he is drunk AND surprised or I wouldn't have him there. I had to reach up to grab his neck. Now I have NO idea what the hell to do. This is not a position I have ever been in before. I am now stone, cold sober, wishing I was drunk.

So I explain to him that I don't like men grabbing my parts and all, and that I'm going to kick his ass if he tries any more stuff, and you know, I'm trying to bluff my way out of this without a black eye. I may have mentioned I don't like black eyes.

So I say "I'm letting you go now" and drop my hand. His hand comes up. I will never know if he was just going to check his neck or what, because at that point I moved through the air. It turns out there are now three guys behind me, ready to defend my honor. How nice. They didn't know me, or anything, just saw a girl in a heap of trouble.

Thanks guys.

Anyway so they just said, "you want to let this go now." And I guess he did, because that was the end of it.

So I decide pool is maybe not the game for me this night, and go back to the regular bar, back to this table. Now do not ask me how I got in a drinking contest. I don't know. Even then I had to have known this is not a smooth move.

Long story short I beat him. This is not because I am great with liquor, or because he is not. It is because I have a strong bladder. I never stood up. He went to the bathroom several times.

So I win my $20, now it is late, and I am going home. Now you leave the club, go down some stairs to the street, and that street leads quickly to my barracks. Easy, right?

Wrong.

Prattle On - Teri Stricker

I got down the steps, I fall in the ditch. I am now realizing just how drunk I truly am. Now these people I was with, mostly guys, followed me. They knew the air might not be so good for me. So they heft me up, another one grabs my purse and camera stuff.

"Leave me alone I don't feel good"

And other foolish things roll out of my mouth. Well they took me home, dropped me in my bed, and left. I remember that. Lord. Anyway they left. I was a lucky girl. Not only did they not take advantage of the mess I put myself in, but took care of my camera stuff too, so I didn't lose it.

The next day was not so hot. I learned the hangover thing. We had a guy in the barracks (men were upstairs, girls downstairs) who liked to hand out religious tracts. He picked this day to knock on my door.

I am sure I looked exactly like I felt because he said. "You look like you need Jesus."

His voice was really loud. My head hurt. A lot. I said "I need to be left alone. Why don't you and Jesus come back some other time?" It was nearly a whisper. So he and Jesus went their way, and I went back to healing.

Like I said, I never drank that much again. It wasn't the hangover. Oh hangovers are bad, but I've had them from nights I didn't even drink much. Didn't even get tipsy. Just used up all the water in my body I guess. No, it was the total lack of control of myself I never wanted to repeat. Having to trust almost strangers to get me home. Anything could have happened. It didn't. I was blessed, and I knew it.

So, throwing men against the wall is not the right way to turn them down, running gets old, and ignoring them doesn't work so good. So now I go back to the drawing board.

I've a love affair with words. I read voraciously. I write awful poems about how I'm alone and loveless and far from home. Maybe words will help here.

So a simple no also does not work. They think you maybe need some convincing. One guy showed me a picture of his fiancé who had died. He thought I looked kind of like her. I thought maybe he was drunker than he thought. He proposed. I said this was not the best idea. Eventually he went back to his beer.

Military men are just like civilian men, just as unique, just as varied. Most can take no for an answer without too much fuss. Most are polite. Well, as polite as one can be propositioning a total stranger. These are not the ones that irritated me so much.

Then there are the ones that just come up and ask. Don't even ask your name. Or other stuff.

Like, this guy buys me a drink. This cost him 80 cents. It's close to closing time, I'm sipping my drink and talking to the bartender. The bartender is used to this, I usually sit up at the bar somewhere near closing time and he sticks by me. He's a nice guy, big Portuguese man who calls me "daughter".

So it's time to go home. I stand up, and the guy who spent the 80 cents asks if he can walk me home. We've been chatting; it's not totally out of the blue. I say no thank you.

So then he comes up with I owe him this walk home (and probably whatever he thinks comes after) because he bought me this drink. So I slap a dollar on the bar, and I tell him that, not to sound conceited or anything, but I think I'm worth more than 80 cents.

So he sits there with his jaw on the bar, the bartender is grinning like a proud father, and I went home.

I should explain. I was at the club a lot. Not a lot else to do when you aren't working. But I didn't actually drink a lot. I nursed my drinks, danced, talked, socialized. Many were the same. I wasn't the only sober person at closing time or anything.

Another night around closing time, a guy who is probably not so rude sober, I don't know walks up to me and asks me if I want to (you know the word). I was feeling creative and full of myself. I admit it. Also wordy.

So I said, "What you are proposing requires two consenting adults, am I right?"

He nods his head in that 'what the hell are you talking about' way folks have when you start using big words. So I said. "Then it will never work, because I'm not consenting, and you are not an adult."

I walked out, didn't look back. Looking back, that would have ruined the drama of the moment. I was in my twenties, it was important then. The bartender later told me the guy had his jaw on the bar for a full minute. He might have been working it out, or I just shocked him. Either way, it worked.

Not all the guys hit on me, of course. I had male friends. Good friends. One guy was a fantastic dancer. He taught me to jitterbug, or at least a version of it. The bar part isn't the only part of the club, there's another section for the band and the dancing, and there's a little room with slot machines, and of course the restaurant I told you about.

He was good to talk to and to dance with, and a friend. He didn't chase me, I didn't do the come hither thing. Friends. And of course I didn't hang out with ALL guys, but you know I mostly did.

The girls mostly talked about the guys. And for some reason, you hang out with a girl long enough, she thinks you are after her boyfriend. Remember, we are outnumbered 10 to 1 by the guys, so I still have no idea why a girl thinks HER guy is the one everyone wants. So I didn't hang out with girls so much as a rule. Less drama that way. Drama is only fun when YOU are the creator, I am thinking.

At the age we were, women are all hormones anyway. So are the guys, I suppose.

So that was the Azores. We worked hard, we played hard. Like good old boys, I guess! Like I said, I wound up pregnant. I fancied myself in love, and I think so did he at the time. Pregnancy changes things, and so does distance, I got transferred. I was supposed to go to Puerto Rico, actually, until I got the news the rabbit died. There was some trouble over there, so they changed my orders. They transferred me to Winter Harbor, Maine. Where I met DAD.

So see? Things happen for a reason. Anyway, eventually we got out of the Navy, got married, happily after ever and all that.

I bet you guessed it's time to chapter again. I bet the happily ever after was a clue. Anyway it is, so let's do it.

Prattle On - Teri Stricker
Chapter Seventeen – True Love and Stuff

By the way, I'm glad you are still here! I mean I can talk to myself and all, it's just not nearly as satisfying.

After I was married and mothering and all, being friends with women came easier. That and probably getting older helps too. Less of the competition thing going on. My best friend in the world is my husband. DAD. That's why I married him.

I think that's why we've done these 21 years. Love is wonderful, I adore DAD. But I really think it's the friendship that has held us together through the years. I don't know if you know this, you probably do, but you can love someone without actually liking them. I don't know why that is, but it's true. I LIKE DAD. He's smart, he's funny, he's talented, what's not to like? He played the piano at Carnegie Hall twice. He was six years old the second time. He's a genius, but I don't hold that against him or anything.

Am I bragging about my man? Well, yeah. I don't think that's a bad thing, is it?

And unless he's been keeping a huge secret for a long time, he LIKES me. He respects my opinions, listens when I speak, brags about me behind my back. Sometimes in front of my back.

I didn't start out a confident person. In fact, I had long pauses in my sentences. It drove DAD nuts. I worked hard at saying the right things. I didn't want to look stupid. The problem is, all that stuff I edited out was ME. So people didn't know me. Not really.

DAD was married when I met him. So the romance thing was an accident. Love grew out of friendship, in other words. He transferred out with his wife before things got out of hand, and we wrote letters, like friends do.

Eventually he got divorced, because although he was great, and his wife was great, they weren't great TOGETHER. It happens. So when he got out of the Navy he came to visit me, and we could admit the love thing.

My poor mother. See, she was a smart lady, but she had just been diagnosed as a manic – depressive. They call it bipolar these days, same thing. Anyway so, they hadn't got her medications quite right as yet, so concentrating was hard. The woman I grew up knowing wasn't there. Her voice wasn't as strong and confident or anything. But I digress.

Again.

So he called. My mom had an unlisted number so he had to go through the operator. I am off at work. Now I don't even know he's out of the Navy and not in Guam anymore. So I come home from work.

"Someone called you collect from California. I didn't accept the charges."

Um. Ok. I had no idea who would call me collect. From California.

Anyway that wasn't exactly what happened. He told her to have me call HIM collect. It was the medications.

Either he didn't hear my mother's end of the conversation, they were going through the operator after all, or my mother sounds like me. He thought it was me, at any rate. So a week later I get a letter, an unhappy letter saying that I could have let the call through and told me I didn't want to see him myself. But he put his number in the letter.

So I called. We talked. He came to visit. I found him a hotel. It all worked.

The thing is I don't think I ever got through to my mother that I had not JUST met this man. To her it was this whirlwind romance and within a few months we were married. She died young, she was only 50 when she went. I think she thought to her dying day that it was love at first sight and I married in haste, thus would repent in leisure.

OR she thought I married him for his money. Which was wrong, and wrong. The first wrong is, I'm just a tad bit more moral than that. Marrying someone for financial gain is wrong, and just not nice. The second wrong is, he wasn't rich. I suppose he looked that way to a woman who worked her tail off for her whole life and hadn't been on a vacation for 20 years. But I don't think she thought that. She'd have said. She didn't mince words.

So he's my best friend. I've now lived longer with DAD than I lived with my parents. Either one of them. The only person who ever knew me better was my mother, and she's been gone since 1990. He knows me, warts and all, and he's still here.

Anyway, all this rambling I do. He's used to it. All I was setting out to say is that you cannot stay insecure and unconfident when you are married to a man like this. I wake up to things like "Good morning gorgeous".

He actually really believes I am smart, and funny, and sing pretty good. I'd have never had the nerve to step on a stage without his support, his utter confidence in me. He is that trite thing you hear about. The love of my life. My best friend. All that stuff.

Now, don't get me wrong, I'm not Shania Twain. I think I said. I don't even want to be. I have sung at bars, a few VFWs, you know, a bar band singer. But even that much would have been beyond me when I was young.

Success breeds confidence as well, of course. People didn't find me funny then. Like I said, I edited out the funny not to look stupid. So you know how people say they would want to be young again? No thanks. I just got comfortable in my own skin somewhere around thirty. I'll stick with stepping into middle age, I'm much better at it.

So DAD and me, we cruise along together nicely. I don't think I've done as much for him has he has for me in the confidence or emotional area, but then he didn't NEED as much of that. It's enough that we've grown together through the years, and not apart.

Prattle On - Teri Stricker

I can't tell you exactly how to make a marriage work, but I can give a few hints. They are kind of obvious though. Like first you pick the right spouse. This is one of the hardest parts. I was engaged like seven times, I know.

The love thing, that's easy. But if you are not also friends, I don't know how lasting it is. It helps if you have some of the same interests. DAD and I both are into music, technology, things like that. He is a history lover. I have gotten to appreciate history more, but I'm still not totally into it. It's enough.

Back when we got married, I used to think, what do people talk about after 20 years? I mean, haven't you said it all?

Nope. Let me set your mind at ease, you never run out of things to talk about. Life is fluid. Things are constantly changing, and so there is plenty to talk about. Plus your kids, what they are doing, what you think of what they are doing.

Communication, learning to compromise, I'm sure you have heard of these things. They work.

Okay, I'm happy, and you are bored. Sorry, I do go on, don't I? Time to chapter and think up another topic.

Chapter Eighteen – General Drivel

Fifty odd pages of drivel. I'm thinking you are fond of drivel. This helps.

So you know more about me than I actually planned on telling. I'm just talking here. It's okay, I'm pretty sure I've nothing to hide. I haven't robbed a bank in my past, I didn't sell my body on street corners, I'm pretty boring as a rule.

Now I'll tell you something about ONLINE. You meet people with nicknames. Some of the nicknames are funny. You rarely know their real names, and almost never their last names. This is ok. I mean does it change the conversations if you know their name, address and phone number? I don't think so.

ONLINE is also nice because you can keep in touch with old friends, with family that doesn't live nearby. I don't much like the phone, I never did. I'm not sure why. My mother didn't either though.

She and my uncle used their kids to talk. No, not kidding. Here's an example. The phone rings.

"Teri, get that."

I pick up the phone. "Hello." Well, you know that IS what you say.

"Hi, this is COUSIN. Dad wants to know what Aunt S is doing tomorrow."

They'd have complete conversations through us without leaving their seats. Now, obviously sometimes they actually talked to each other. Like when us kids were the subject, or we were all at school or something. So I guess I don't come by the not liking the phone thing strangely.

I E-mail. I don't use AOL so I don't get the "You got mail." I get "DING". I can change that, but really the ding is shorter. It irritates me for a shorter time, you see?

Prattle On - Teri Stricker

Before ONLINE I wrote letters. The problem is I wrote lots of letters, and rarely sent them. My Dad don't hear from me much because they are not ONLINE and I still don't send them as often as I should.

My Dad was always cool. He was stylin'. He was handsome, he was smart, he chased his dreams. He didn't dream of being an astronaut or anything. His dreams were actually quite simple. He wanted to live off the land, for example. He wanted to live like our ancestors did. So he got a cabin up in northern Michigan. No electricity. He had a generator for the evening news, I don't think he turned it on other than that. Naturally my stepmother had to agree to all this, I mean this is not always easy, this sort of living.

They had a wood stove for heat, they had another one for cooking.

He wanted to do it and he did it. He wasn't rich. He just did it. My stepmother managed the money so that they COULD do that.

After a few years, he decided he'd done it, and they moved on.

I told you, he is cool.

Me, I don't have dreams like that. I like electricity and central air. But going to visit him was fun for a day or two.

And, I like my ONLINE.

My husband he likes the television. He likes to even sleep to it. I can't sleep with it on unless I'm really tired. So he'll start snoring, I turn it off.

Oops too fast.

"HEY! I was WATCHING that."

"How could you hear it over your snoring?"

"Well I'm awake NOW, so turn it on."

Okay. Eventually I learned the gradual turn it down trick. This doesn't shock him into waking up. THEN the power. It works.

He watches the news a lot. With cable you can find out what drivel is happening at any time of the day. He likes to tell me. I don't usually like to know. This is why I don't watch TV. News is depressing. They don't tell you nice things. How Jane Doe got on the honor roll. They tell you about riots and people dying.

It's okay, DAD keeps up with it all for me. If we have to take cover he'll tell me.

He even wakes me up to tell me things. 3 AM he wakes me up to tell me Ray Charles died. I like Ray Charles. He had soul.

So I blink in the light and say. "Well you think he'll still be dead tomorrow?"

DAD rolls his eyes. With good reason. But really what can I do? Ray Charles was a great singer, and as far as I know, a good man. He died. I'm sorry. But I don't really KNOW Ray Charles. We didn't visit. I didn't have coffee with him at Starbucks. I can't call his family and comfort them. I can just sit there in bed and feel sad. I could have felt sad tomorrow, this is all I am saying.

Yep, you are right. Chapter time. It's not so exciting anymore, but it has to be done all the same.

Chapter Nineteen – Stuff about Stuff

Death is awful. I hate it. I never want to do it. Of course, I will someday, I'm not immortal or anything. But me dying, well, I won't know, will I?

Other people dying, I have to deal with that. We all do. People we love, they die. It sucks. It either brings families together, or it tears them apart.

When my mother died, she didn't have so much to fight over. It was ok. I set out everything I thought I needed to remember her by, and BROTHER, he nodded wisely. There were no arguments about anything, and certainly not about STUFF.

We are obsessed with STUFF in this country. I've noticed. We have to have STUFF. Shiny, new STUFF. I don't know why. I like my STUFF. But it's only so important, you know?

The computers are our work and our play. My business is ONLINE, mostly, though I go out and fix computers sometimes. My husband makes web sites for people. We rarely have to go out into the world to do these things. We go out into the ONLINE world. We can make a web site for someone across the country and never meet them face to face. Some folks, they want the face to face, so if those folks are far away, then we don't do their site that's all.

The passing of information is so easy now. You can write drivel like I am doing without white-out, or the noise of a typewriter. I can copy this paragraph and put it way up in the first chapter if I want to. I don't want to. But I CAN.

Then there's my guitar, my mixer, my microphone. STUFF. There's other STUFF, the knick knacks, furniture, you know, STUFF. But although we need some STUFF, it doesn't have to be our whole life, accumulating more STUFF. George Carlin covered the whole STUFF issue pretty well, I think. I'm just saying, don't put your heart and soul into STUFF.

Prattle On - Teri Stricker

I used to collect autographs. You go to the concert, you stand in the line. They sign a picture for you. It's nice. The autograph, it goes in a box. You might look at it twice in 20 years. So after a while I quit with the autographs.

Some people collect other things. It's okay. They are allowed. As long as they aren't collecting someone else's things. That would be bad.

I just had to answer the door. They wanted to give me stuff. See how that works? They were Jehovah's Witnesses. Don't cringe, they are nice people. I just don't happen to be one. I told them I wasn't interested, they went away. Simple.

Some people, they talk to them for 30 minutes, take the literature and wonder why they come back. Well you encouraged them, that's all.

I've studied with them. They are smart people. They can take no for an answer, but you have to tell them no. They believe they need to spread the WORD. They aren't the only ones, you know. Until you tell them no, I'm not interested, it's like their JOB to tell you about it.

I have friends who are Witnesses. They don't worship the devil or anything. You talk with them, they aren't going to sacrifice your first born. They just will not tell you what you want to hear. They tell you the truth as they see it, that's all.

People hide from them. This sounds to me like a confidence problem. I've never had a problem with them leaving if I say I don't want to talk. I'm not sure what the hiders think is going to happen. They might be sucked into being a Witness against their will? I don't know, I'm just you know, theorizing.

GOD is outlawed in this country. At least that's what it seems like. I told you way back about JESUS being sent home from school. I'm not heavily into the religion thing. I don't need to have GOD plastered all over the place, that's not what I mean.

But you know, they want Him out of everything. They want "Under God" out of the pledge of allegiance even. He can't go to school, He can't be anywhere near anything referring to the government, some folks balk at the Christmas nativity scenes even.

I don't get it. I just don't think it's that big a deal. I grew up, Jesus was around. The nativity scenes on lawns, all lit up. Pretty. They're kind of expressing their opinion that way.

And, isn't that what Christmas is about? UM that's why it's CHRISTmas and not SANTAmas. You see what I'm saying? Everyone doesn't celebrate Christmas, that's okay. The Jewish folks have Hanukkah, this is good. I don't see a problem here, except the one folks are making.

You are telling me that a scene on a lawn is going to force you to go to their church? What? Maybe you can explain this to me.

The founding fathers didn't have these problems. Most of them believed in God, and kinda liked the big guy. They just didn't want their government to come up with a state religion. They didn't want the ten commandments to be in the constitution. That kind of thing.

Now see this is kinda politics. AND religion. I said I wasn't going to do that. Of course I also said I might change my mind. So I guess we're okay.

I don't want people pushing their religion on me either, I just think we've gone NUTS that's all. Way way back everyone had to believe in GOD and go to the state church, and people died and stuff over it. That was bad. I don't think a picture of Jesus or something is going to take us back to that that's all.

I was taught history. We had a class. World History. We learned the two theories. The theory of creation, and the theory of evolution. We read Genesis, or part of it anyway. I bet they don't do that NOW. My goodness there'd be a riot.

Now they teach the big bang like it's a fact. They proved it when I wasn't looking? That could happen, like I say, I don't watch the news.

The other part is, the bible says God created the earth. Then the stuff, then the critters and man. It doesn't tell us how. There's not a step by step manual or anything. So you know, it could all be one thing. I don't know. Now this is assuming there's God. If there's not God, well then, ok. Either way, it's all very mysterious how we got here.

Don't you think so?

But I'm thinking soon we'll have to go to the bad part of town, knock on a door, and say a password to get in and buy our Christmas balls.

Well I have hit both taboo subjects and the lightning hasn't struck. This is good. I hate that. So let's chapter before I get myself in real trouble.

Prattle On - Teri Stricker
Chapter Twenty – Hunting and All

I grew up with a father who liked to hunt, and fish. I've eaten a lot of stuff that would probably make you go "ew."

I've had rabbit and squirrel and venison and bear. I've eaten Possum. I've eaten Raccoon. I'm not fond of bear, very strong flavor.

Anyway, now we have the tree huggers. I use this term because you will know who I mean. These people want us to stop hunting and fishing and all.

Conservation is good, don't get me wrong. But many of these people tell us that we are OUTSIDE of nature. HELLO? We are the top of the food chain. Unless of course a lion catches us, then they are.

They also don't understand hunting. It's cruel and all. Now, I grew up with a hunting father. It was meat. We ate it. I don't think the trophy hunting is all that great if you aren't eating what you kill. That's the rule, you eat what you kill. That is what the hunting is for. Food. They have arcade games and shooting ranges for just playing with your gun.

The lion kills the antelope, or whatever is over there, he eats it. He doesn't chop off its head and mount it on his wall and let the meat rot. You can mount the head on your wall, I don't care; just don't waste the meat. This is all I'm saying.

Then there are trees. They are important. I agree. They now cut down trees and they plant more. They didn't always. But now they do. So we have wood to make things. We have paper and all. So that you can read my drivel in the bathroom. And the trees are there to make our air happy. All good.

Animals have gone extinct since we have gone industrial. This is our fault. See, I'm not so sure of that. Animals went extinct before we went industrial. In fact, dinosaurs went extinct before we were even HERE. So you know it may not be ALL about us. We are rather conceited, I've noticed.

Prattle On - Teri Stricker

I don't think replenishing what we take is wrong. I don't think worrying about the critters is wrong. I just think that there's a middle ground. People don't want folks to hunt deer, for example. No more venison.

On the face of it, you can see their point. We have beef and pork and stuff. By the way beef, pork, and stuff, this comes from animals. There isn't a factory somewhere that manufactures it. They are just not wandering in the wild is all.

But they don't know what happens when you stop. See, the thing is, deer have children, and then THEY have children, and on and on. Fawns they call them. You know, like Bambi.

Bambi is cute. I wouldn't shoot Bambi unless I was REAL hungry. Anyway. So now the deer population goes up. The predators are at the same level, except we took MAN out of the equation. The available food, this also stays the same.

So what happens is the deer starve. This is not a fun way to die. They wander into the roads on their hunts for food more often, and so more cars hitting deer.

They wander into your gardens too, because there is food there. You can't blame them. But people are growing that food for themselves, not for the deer. They get upset.

What people forget is the law of the jungle. Survival of the Fittest. The lions can eat the deer, but we can't? No fair!

Animals also adapt. Look at the rat. He is very healthy, Mr. Rat. He's everywhere whether we like it or not. Once upon a time, Mr. Rat's kind lived in the wild. Shoot, once we did too.

He adapted.

Now I'm not saying that we should go out and clear all the land and get all the critters condos. I'm just saying that once again, people are going crazy. There's a middle ground to every argument and fewer and fewer folks can find it.

Prattle On - Teri Stricker

Caring is good. I love caring. I love people. I love caring people. Radicals, I'm not so fond of.

Doesn't matter the flavor of the radical, they are nuts. Radical, extremist, same thing.

Many don't apply a lot of logic to their positions. Logic is important folks. Try building a house without some logic. It doesn't work.

Also some knowledge doesn't hurt. I mean, like I'm logical, but I STILL can't build a house. I don't know HOW. I could learn, but right this minute, no clue.

GIRL is a radical, extremist toe nail clipper. She clips them puppies to the quick. You know what happens? She gets ingrown toenails. That hurts. Then they get infected, that's not healthy. EXTREME is not healthy, see?

Also extreme eating is not good, gives you a bellyache. Do it every day and you get fat. Your arteries clog up. You see?

So, just you know, think a little. Thinking is a good thing. Just don't do it all at once, you get a headache.

I don't know what it is but people are yelling a lot more. It might be that respect thing. THEY know what is good for us, we are idiots. Sometimes, they are right, I admit it. But I am an American, I am allowed to be an idiot.

Smoking is a big thing now. It used to be a smoker said "do you mind if I smoke?" and if you minded, you said so. They smoked elsewhere.

NOW, they want everyone to quit no matter where they are. Some places smoking outside is even bad. That puff of smoke is going to kill the planet or something.

I am an idiot, I smoke. I admit it. I don't smoke where I am not supposed to. Even at home, I smoke outside. I use ashtrays. If there are no ashtrays I have a container I carry for my butts. Easy.

I guess maybe not so easy because I see butts EVERYWHERE. Next to ashtrays and garbage cans even. Yeah, I don't get it either, and I smoke. I think we're back to the lack of respect thing.

You can't smoke in the hospital. I plan to die at home. I'm going to be miserable enough without you take away my cigarettes and make me go into withdrawal.

Every so often, I try to quit. I'm not good at it. It's not a talent I have. DAD quit ages ago. He had the talent.

Chapter time. Yep I think so. You know the drill, come on along.

Chapter Twenty One – Happiness 101 or Something

Twenty one. That seems so young now doesn't it? Unless you are that age range, I suppose. Twenty one was an anti-climax for me. I could already drink; you remember that Navy ID was my ticket to beer. I'd left home a few years before. So you know, there was no THING I could do to mark it.

It's okay, really, I survived. I didn't feel like I was so young. In some ways I was older at 21 than I am now. I've learned to relax. It's not ALL so hard anymore.

So how to be happy? I mean not just a happy moment here and there, but really BE a happy person. I'm a happy person, it's a talent I have. I can tell you a few things, but I don't know how easy they are to follow. I'm not you, after all.

Turn OFF the television once in a while. It's full of bad news. It's full of those commercials that make you feel like you aren't worthwhile if you don't buy their stuff. It's full of those soap operas.

I told you BOY has GIRLfriend. She is not happy. She is stressed. Often. She has a job, okay, I get that. She goes to school. Got it. Many happy people do the same things without a problem. So I watch what she is doing one day.

She watches soap operas. Then at night she watches dramas. She watches that channel where they have the weepy movies.

No WONDER she is stressed. Turn the channel, watch a comedy. Watch something wonderfully stupid. Quit borrowing manufactured stress. Better yet, turn OFF the TV. Read a book, take a ride, and maybe exercise. Macramé, do SOMETHING.

This book, it's wonderfully stupid, right? You are already reading it, so you've taken the first step. See how easy that is?

Then there's the things you can't change. World Hunger. The war overseas. Let go of them. Relax. I realize this is not easy. But there is nothing you can do, if there was, you would be doing it. So set your mind to solvable problems. A crossword maybe.

I should mention here that I'm not a shrink. Nope. I haven't even played one on TV. This is just how I stay happy. It may not work for you, but it won't hurt to try it if you are not happy a lot.

Some people live in the past. Bad things happened. Mistakes were made. Me too. My childhood wasn't full of fluffy clouds either. I made lots and lots of mistakes, like that guy against the wall. CHILDREN now, they aren't mistakes, they are happy accidents.

So here we are in the past. It sucks. You got to let it go. Not easy. Your mind won't let it go until you can forgive some people, maybe even yourself. Also not easy. But if you don't do it you're dragging that past with you and it is damn heavy.

Take my past. Well, you probably don't want it. Anyway like I said in an earlier chapter, My mom was a manic – depressive – bipolar in today-speak. She didn't suddenly become that after I grew up that's just when they figured it out.

Also, she was an alcoholic. The alcoholic part is why they didn't figure out the bipolar. It hid it. I look back I don't see the glorious highs and horrific lows. The beer covered it.

Anyway so it was not wine and roses. It was beer and thorns, but there were roses striving in there too.

I analyze things to death. I'm like my Dad like that. Maybe he taught me. I don't think it's bad; he's a happy person too.

So. Analyze time. This woman who bore me, she didn't set out to make me miserable. She didn't look at me in the receiving blanket and say "I'm going to make sure this kid thinks she's a piece of shit." She didn't DO that. It just happened.

Prattle On - Teri Stricker

You know, there's not a lot of training in the parenting department. We have no clue. They have some classes these days, I hear, but they had nothing when my mother had me.

So. She sets out to teach me right from wrong, house train me, that stuff. Meanwhile life is not always kind to her, and she's an addictive personality besides. Somewhere along the way she becomes a chain smoking alcoholic.

The things she said that weren't so nice, she thought might piss me off and make me try harder. Sometimes it could have been just frustration. The point is just that her intentions were good.

No, that didn't change the result. It didn't give me those fluffy cloud memories. But I've some good ones anyway, from childhood, and lots of them after I grew up. My point is that she didn't set out to do this. Misery loves company, and she was pretty miserable.

So I understand, she didn't mean it. So the next step is forgiveness. This isn't about God or finding my way to heaven, this is about getting on with my life. So I forgave her. She was human, poor thing.

I forgave her long ago, when I was young, and she was still alive. I forgave her while she was still throwing the insults. They didn't hurt so much after that.

After she quit drinking, she cried in my arms and said she was sorry. I told her it was ok. And it is. We moved on.

We got close after that. My phone bills were awful until she died. I miss her. The phone company misses her. But you know, we go on.

She was never happy. She never let go of anything. Her mistakes, the things that happened to her, she never let go. So it's a lesson. Let go.

That's the serious part. I wanted to share that, because I want people to be happy. I don't know how easy that is, it came naturally to me. I didn't set out to do it, I didn't go to a shrink and lay on a couch, it just happened.

Prattle On - Teri Stricker

Now, take a look around you. This whole book, it's about life. Sorta.

For example, ducks. Many years ago, I told you, we lived by a lake. The lake has ducks. People lived across from the lake in places along the road, and they fed the ducks. Now the ducks are crossing the street.

DAD and I didn't mind. We drive up, the ducks want to cross so we sit and watch them waddle across. They didn't take an hour or anything, just a minute or two. Then we'd drive on.

Sometimes we are behind someone who doesn't see it that way. They honk, they yell.

The ducks STOP. They are scared. After a minute of terror, they continue. This someone who honked, he SLOWED THEM DOWN. This means he or she had to wait LONGER for them to cross. They are nervous now and cautious. And slow. The screaming and the honking did nothing for the driver OR the ducks. Think about that.

Honking in stalled traffic. This also fixes nothing. Turn up the radio and sing to it or something. You can't do anything to speed it up, so you might as well relax.

I've a friend who is a stress queen. She can wear you out. She doesn't mean to, but she is just so stressed it is an effort not to get stressed with her.

So we are in her car, going to her house. We don't have an appointment. I'm going to fix her computer, but I'm not charging for travel time. So we hit the intersection. It is tourist season. She is stressing. Muttering words under her breath. Next to her is an Arby's bag, and of course, me.

So I say, eat. Relax. Eventually we'll move. I don't have a curfew.

A sense of humor helps. It does. Things that upset you, I might laugh at. If I can I will find a way to laugh at it. Like the lines in Walmart.

Stressing doesn't HELP. I'm telling you it won't make that line move faster. So you might as well talk to the person in front of or behind you. You might like them. Or look at the magazines, those are funny. You don't have to even pick them up. Especially the Enquirer.

So the doorbell again. Speaking of funny. The doorbell hasn't rung in at least a week now it's twice in 3 hours. This time it's the Mormons. I'm not upset I had to go up the stairs, unlock the door and talk to them. What's the problem? They are people. I am people, they wanted to talk.

I came down and said to DAD "First the Witnesses, now the Mormons, who is next?"

Life is funny, I'm telling you.

It's hard sometimes, life. The money problems, the people problems. I know, I have a life too. But, it is just also funny.

Next time you go to work, pay attention to what is going on at break time. Or at lunch. Humor happens all around you, you just have to see it.

So that's the don't worry be happy chapter. Are we happy yet?

Yes, time to chapter. You are really good at this.

Prattle On - Teri Stricker
Chapter Twenty Two – Words You Can't Use

So we are now happy, even though there is no world peace and the cable bill is still due next week.

The Witnesses and the Mormons went home. DAD is planning dinner and here I am, with you. Now we have to decide what to talk about. Or you know, drivel about.

I love words. I think I said. But you know, there are some that you just, can't use. And plenty we can. I'll explain. Why not? It's a book. Books have words in them. So, here we go.

Antidisestablishmentarianism for example. It's a really cool word. But where the hell do we put it? It'll take five minutes to say that word, for one thing. Put that in a sentence you've just hogged the conversation, and the others are looking at you funny.

"Anti WHAT?" Now you have to say it again. So, you can't use it. It's still a great word.

Chortle. It rolls off the tongue, doesn't it? Here's the definition; Chortle is a portmanteau word (also known as a blend) that combines the words "chuckle" and "snort." It was coined by Lewis Carroll in the nonsense poem Jabberwocky, which appeared in the book Through the Looking-Glass (1872)

Portmanteau, that's a neat word we never hear too, come to think of it.

WAY cool word. However, I've never heard a soul use it in conversation. I have seen it in books, there it works. Of course that portmanteau, that's pretty too. Also unusable in a real live conversation.

I was a kid who wanted to sound smart. I used big words. BROTHER called them ten dollar words. People got mad; they needed a dictionary to talk to me. I also thought the British accent was intelligent sounding, so I tried that. I wasn't very good at it. I sounded kinda like Daffy Duck, drunk.

Prattle On - Teri Stricker

Ineluctable. Gorgeous word, isn't it? It means Inevitable or unavoidable. Still can't use it. Me and you, we're the only people outside of the dictionary makers that know what it means.

Flibbertigibbet. I love it. It even LOOKS funny. It is A silly, scatterbrained person. Just like you probably thought it meant. We all know at least one of those. The things is, can't use it. Even if everyone knows the word. Because the person you are calling that is going to get upset. Dang.

Hullabaloo. I like this word, it rolls off the tongue. And we can even use it. We will get funny looks, I admit, but we can use it. And even better it is exactly what you think it is. A commotion.

Euphonious. Sounds like a crime, doesn't it? He committed a Euphonious assault. But no, it means Pleasant sounding, especially a pleasant sounding word. Like Euphonious, for example. It flows off the tongue. Of course you say, "Marge your name is Euphonious." She might slap you before you have the time to explain.

You know, we don't use a lot of big words when we talk, not even the easy ones.

Take impeccable. We know what it means. We don't use it. In fact if I think about most of the conversations I have, we don't use many words over six letters at all.

If you are communicating that's not bad, I just noticed.

Corpulent. We've seen it in books. COOL word. We don't use it though. Obese or fat is shorter.

Some people are in a hurry to spit out what they have to say. They are afraid we will interrupt them. The people who do this are also the ones who will interrupt you while you are speaking. Maybe you noticed this too.

This book is basically a one-sided conversation isn't it? I just thought of that. Wow. Normal conversation shouldn't be. When you have finished speaking, don't rush to think of what to say next, it should be natural. Listen to what the other conversationalist is saying. It might be funny. It might impart wisdom. You don't know unless you listen.

Now, I sound all knowing up there, but I do it too. I think of a funny line or something and I forget to listen. I'm not Ms. Perfect, you know. These things I say to remind myself as well.

I'm about to digress again, are you ready?

I just read some of this over, this drivelly book, and I realize something. I'm writing in the voice of like, all the Jewish comics I've ever heard, or read. Now. I gotta ask myself, do I think I'm a Jewish comic?

Really. I'm not kidding. The Maybe this and Maybe that. Also, the alsos. I LIKE it, don't get me wrong. I'm just wondering where it is coming from because I'm not a comic, and I'm pretty sure I'm not Jewish. It seems to be working, and I'm in Chapter twenty two already, kinda late to change now. Maybe it's because I'm typing. Maybe my fingers are Jewish. Or comical. I don't know. I just noticed.

Cogitate. Wonderful word, hard to use. It means some heavy thinking. But I've never found myself saying, "QUIET! I'm trying to cogitate here!" I'm betting you haven't either.

Transmogrify – love it. Beautiful word. Useless. Unless you are talking about a movie like "The Fly" or something. Not likely to come up in conversation, as a rule. Darn it.

Heterodoxy – fantastic, rolls off the tongue. Again, useless. Kinda like unorthodox except that it can only be used about religion. Sigh. Another one bites the dust.

Frenzy – It's not a big word, you can use it, but I LIKE it. It's just a great word to say. Say it with me Frennnnnnzy. See?

Feisty – Usable and fun. I'm feisty, right? You can disagree; I won't go into a frenzy or anything.

Well, the coffee cup is empty, my butt is asleep, and I think I it's time to chapter. You should probably stretch or something, too, right?

So. Chapter time. We should have some cool music or something huh? We'll call it "Chapter Time Waltz"

Prattle On - Teri Stricker
Chapter Twenty Three – Familial Bliss or Not?

You know, at this point, even I am surprised to still be typing. I mean, I realize I have always liked to talk. I realize I am a person full of drivel. But even I didn't know I had this much drivel stored inside, just waiting to burst out.

I mentioned earlier, I've a cat. TC. He is a nice cat. He sheds, I vacuum, this is not a big problem. But he has interesting idiosyncrasies, you see. Oh there's one of those very cool words, huh? But it is true. I cannot have a normal pet, he must be eccentric.

Most cats, a door is ajar, they will nudge it open, or even lift a paw and pull it open. Not TC. He will stand there and meow at it until YOU open it.

Then there is the eating thing. He likes to eat, but more importantly, he needs to know the food is THERE. He gets very upset if he can see any part of the bottom of the bowl.

There is plenty of food in there, he will not starve, but there is a centimeter of blue shining through. So, I must stir it up and cover that centimeter. I call it the "blue bowl syndrome", because his bowl is blue.

Also he will lead me to a full food dish. Yes. He will stand wherever I may be, and meow until I tell him "show me."

Sometimes he leads me to the door to the world, but usually it is to the bowl. Which is full. Of food.

My theory is, he is lazy. He wants to go eat, but, the bowl MIGHT be empty. You don't know. So he leads me. This way, if it happens to be empty, he doesn't have to make the long trek to me to lead me to his empty bowl.

This is my cat. Perhaps I am a bad influence, I don't know.

I was just talking to another friend ONLINE. I know, I know, addiction to online. This is okay, I mean, it gives me more drivel. We were discussing pregnancy.

So of course, I must now talk about it. Pregnancy is sometimes harder on the father than on the mother, I have noticed.

You tell your spouse there is a little package on the way. We'll say spouse. I know there is not always a spouse. I have GIRL, her father and I were not wed, but let's say for this drivel, there is a spouse.

So you tell your husband there is a package on the way. This is a happy time, in my scenario I am painting. We will avoid the "Oh my God this is awful" scenario, that one is not funny.

I'm digressing again. We'll go to my first pregnancy a moment. I was in the Navy for this, you remember?

I was given a light duty order by my doctor. On the form it said something like "disability or DISEASE" So my GIRL, until she was born, was either a disability or a disease. I have not told her. It could traumatize her for life, being called a disease, don't you think? Okay, let's go back to the normal drivel, rather than the personal drivel.

So, back to the married couple who has just learned they are pregnant. THEY truly are. The man does not get out of this unscathed you know. He is now married to a hormonal BOMB. It could go off any minute. And frequently does.

So the new father to be says. "Sit down! Can I get you anything?" Suddenly his wife is a piece of blown glass. She likes this, but of course she cannot admit it. So she tells him how she is just fine and does not need to sit down quite yet.

We leave them happily celebrating. He has wine, she has some fruit juice, a happy scene.

Fast forward. Why are we in the bathroom? Morning sickness. Oh dear. This is one of the not so fun parts of bringing junior into the world.

In the bedroom adjoining this bathroom sits our father to be, looking a little green in the gills himself. He is wondering what he should do. There is nothing. I am sorry. I know, it is hard to be useless, but in this instance all you can really do is commiserate. This stage will pass, you know.

Meanwhile, father to be is learning to be cautious. The hormones are simply RAGING. There is no way to know, each time he sees her, just what her mood will be. One moment she is smiling, the woman he fell in love with, and the next she wants to rip his heart out because he left the seat up in the bathroom.

He also finds himself dressing and going to the store because she needs ketchup. She needs it NOW. She cannot eat her ice cream and dill pickles without it, can't he SEE that?

No, he cannot. His hormones are not raging. His abdomen is not distended, and he does not have these cravings. However, he knows there will be no sleeping, and so he is going as quickly as he can.

Drive safely. By the time you return she'll need something else.

Fast forward.

Mother feels now like a beached whale. Sitting down and standing up has become an art form. She will not believe her husband still find her beautiful. He does. He is awed by this whole process.

Both are terrified. Soon will come this screaming gorgeous baby into their lives. They have taken the breathing classes, and have done everything that they can do to get ready. The nursery is painted. The crib has been assembled three times.

We think it is right now, it no longer rocks back and forth when touched. Father to be has tested it with the dog. The dog didn't mind, he just thought it was a little odd. The dog is a German Shepherd.

Prattle On - Teri Stricker

In the drawers of this adorable room are adorable tiny clothes. We have learned this child will be a girl. Everything is pink and lacy.

They do not know, though they have been told, that within two weeks of birth, all of these things will be stained with spit up. So will all of their clothes. They will learn.

Fast Forward.

We are in a birthing room. Mom is a bit cranky. She has been in labor 20 hours. The nurse is constantly adjusting the monitor straps around her belly. The nurse is good, not one of Mom's slaps has touched her. She must have been good at dodge ball.

Father to be can not stay sitting down. It doesn't matter that it has been 20 hours and his back and feet hurt, he can't sit down. The doctor tells us it will still be a while.

21 hours. He sits down. He has said "You are doing great honey!" exactly 1,435 times. He is now bored. He turns on the TV.

"TURN THAT $%*%&%&% THING OFF!!!! How can you watch TV when I am DYING here?"

He turns off the TV. He sits.

For the next two hours, his wife is the daughter of Satan. He is hearing words he was never sure she even knew. He is everything but a good person. It is okay father, this is transition. This is why the nurse is smiling. The end is in sight.

After much ado, Now comes the baby. Screaming. This is good. This means the lungs are working. You will hear them working a lot in the next few months. This is quiet. Wait until she strengthens them a little.

Fast Forward.

This is the first night home. Mother in law is here, advising. Half of the known universe is in the living room. Happiness abounds.

Prattle On - Teri Stricker

The sun sets on a wonderful day. The people go home, even mother in law. The baby is sleeping, the parents go to bed. Smiling.

Until 2 AM. Baby is screaming. She does not want food, cuddling is not working. So now we pace. By 6 AM we are ready to scream with baby. We dial Mother in law. We get the number wrong three times.

Mother in law says lay her in your lap belly down and burp her. She was expecting your call. She got up at 5 AM. She has 5 other grandchildren, she is ready.

So you quickly do this. Baby farts, baby burps, baby spits up on the nightgown. Before you can finish wiping up, baby sleeps.

Aaaah. Relief.

Father has to go to work. He looks like a zombie, but he still must go. They have responsibilities after all. They have to pay for baby's college. Slow down father, first the diapers.

The day goes by. The new father fell asleep in a meeting. They understand. They see the circles, they know he is a new father.

He comes home.

No Kiss. No "How was your day?"

No, not at all. What he gets is. "I am a terrible mother! Why did you do this to me?"

Oh dear.

Mother in law was called 26 times by 10 AM. By then she has gotten Father in law off to work and the housework done, so she just came over for the rest of the day. Things went better for baby, but now the new mother feels like she is the worst mother on the planet.

This is not Mother in law's fault. She is not telling the mother this. She simply knows what to do.

Let us leave now. This is stressful. They will learn, and perhaps soon they will be a happy family. They will have funny stories about this time of their life. They just aren't very funny right this instant.

So yes, friend, it is time to chapter. I like to think you are my friend. I can't drivel all over just anyone you know. So we will chapter and see what is next together.

Prattle On - Teri Stricker
Chapter Twenty Four – The Kitchen

So now we have chaptered twenty three times. We've been through a lot already, you and I. Well, we have if you are still here. Hello? I hear a dial tone. Oh dear.

I am the intrepid drivel mistress, this does not deter me. Onward.

We have examined many aspects of life up to now. We've even examined the bathroom. We've missed the kitchen. I don't know how either. We both have kitchens, why didn't you remind me?

We come through the door. We expect gleaming appliances. A shining floor. A pristine sink. WHY? We should really know better by now. There is the family after all.

In my kitchen there is first the kitchen table. This is supposed to be where we can have a quick breakfast, maybe a food preparation area.

No. It is not.

It is a repository. Right now there are many things on it, none of which actually relate to the kitchen.

First there are toys belonging to GRANDGIRL and GRANDBOY. These are toys that they were playing with in inappropriate manners. For instance, the ball. It looks harmless there on the table, doesn't it? Three lamps have found the floor because of this ball.

GIRL, the mother of these wonderful children, has discovered another child lives in this house. I knew it. It is the same child I had. We never found him, but he is a brat, this child. He has overturned lamps, he has spilled horrible things on nice carpets. He has broken windows.

This is not a nice child.

Although we cannot FIND this child to perhaps put him in timeout, we know his name. It is IDUNNO. You have one of the same name? I am not surprised. There was a sale, maybe.

Prattle On - Teri Stricker

You come into the living room that was clean an hour ago. A tornado you never saw or heard has been here.

"Look at this mess! Who did this?"

BOY; "IDUNNO."

GIRL; "IDUNNO."

We have a consensus. This brat IDUNNO has done this.

So you look at your children, who you love, who could never have done such a thing after they watched you breaking your back cleaning it, and you call out.

"IDUNNO! Come here please!"

Crickets.

GIRL and BOY are used to this, they don't even giggle.

"IDUNNO has left the building. That figures. Well I guess you two are going to have to clean up after him then. Hop to it."

So they clean up in their childlike way. I am sure they are muttering about what they are going to do to IDUNNO when he comes home. I don't think they ever do these things however, because somehow he is back causing trouble in no time.

I digressed again, didn't I? So let us return to the kitchen, and the table.

The harmless ball that has murdered the lamps. It is still there. There is a hammer. I don't know why. Perhaps SLSIL fixed something. He does this sometimes. He does not, however, put the tools away. This is my job. No, I do not know why, but it is.

There are crayons, there are various things. You get the idea. Probably the same things are on your kitchen table. We turn.

The refrigerator. Chocolate handprints. I'm now the Grandmother, well, actually I am NANA and DAD he is now PAPA. So I am NANA not MOM, so before cleaning this, I get the camera. It's adorable. The first 150 times, anyway.

Cleaning the outside of the refrigerator is not as easy at it sounds. There are a thousand magnets. Some hold the grocery list, some hold wonderful artworks by the grandchildren, some are not whole. But eventually it is clean, all the things are redistributed.

Now the cupboards. They are supposed to be white. However now there are lines going down them. Nice pattern. There is the grape juice line, a lovely shade of purple, isn't it? There is the milk line. This is white, just, raised up a bit. There is the Lemonade line. You get the idea. This we just clean.

Now, I am not the only one who cleans these things. This is just today. We are studiously NOT looking at the floor because that comes last in any case. You know this. Clean the floor first and the rest of the cleaning lands on it, and we just have to do it again.

The upper cabinets, just a few handprints, nothing horrible.

Now we look to the counters.

We wish we hadn't. How many days of dishes is this, anyway?

One. No I am not kidding. We are a family of 4 adults and 2 children remember. So we open the dishwasher and load. PAPA, also known as DAD depending on my mood, calls it "Lock and Load." It's more "Load and Lock", but that doesn't sound as good, does it?

And yes, it must be locked. The children like the pretty buttons. I could guard it for the ridiculous amount of time it runs, but this locking the buttons thing makes it unnecessary.

This does not stop them from OPENING the dishwasher, thus stopping the cycle. You cannot just close it, and it starts back up. No. You must Unlock the buttons, click "continue" or whatever that button says, and Relock it. To lock and unlock takes 3 seconds. This can add up, not to mention the time before you discover the open door. So if you want to eat tonight, you keep the grandchildren out of the kitchen.

Prattle On - Teri Stricker

Now you can see the counters. There is peanut butter, jelly, a few unidentifiable things. This is cleanable, and you wonder why it wasn't wiped up at the time.

You go to the sink, and now you know. The dishrag. This has been here since maybe Noah and the flood. I don't know why we didn't smell it from the doorway. So this goes to the hamper and you grab a new one, untouched by grime.

You return to the sink. There is rust. A pile of rust. Oh. The Brillo. Well it was at one time, now it is a pile of rust. So this goes to the garbage, carefully. Remember how I said the floor was last for a reason? This is partly why. Rust particles have to have made it to the floor on my trek to the garbage I am thinking.

Back to the sink. Behind the faucet is filth. And the backsplash is, well, splashed. So the grime free rag is put to use. Eventually we get to the counters.

Did you ever notice how dirty the dish drainer gets? Or the thingy under it? How? I don't know. We are putting CLEAN dishes in it to dry, are we not? Yet it gets filthy all the same. So we clean this too.

The stove tells its own story. You can tell everything that has been cooked on it today, and maybe last night. Something also has burned in the burner pan. Again.

We have not learned, either. We keep replacing them. Someday I will get smart, and keep the new for company. Pull out the discolored horrific things, and put in the new for looks, and do NOT use them. Put the yucky ones back in there when we cook. Voila?

Except you know, we'll forget.

Then there is the floor, and taking out the garbage, and now we have this pristine kitchen we expected to see when we came in.

PAPA comes in followed by the grandchildren. It is lunch time.

It is also time to chapter. The kitchen is clean for about five minutes, and I want to get out of here while I have this picture in my head.

Prattle On - Teri Stricker
Chapter Twenty Five – Familial Stuff

My friends tell me this is like an erma bombeck book. Yes, I did not capitalize, she doesn't why should I? Now I feel bad. I don't think so. Erma bombeck is a real live author. I am a driveling fiend. There is quite a difference.

So I told you earlier, I didn't know how long this should go. So I dug up a book that isn't one of the big fat novels I like to read, you know, to get a clue or something.

Anyway I went to the last page. 255. We have a ways to go yet. I realize I don't have to go to 255. I could have 254, or 256. This is not an exact science, this driveling. But it's a ballpark figure.

I remember enough about erma to know that she talked a lot about her family. I'm talking about my family. I hope she doesn't have a copyright on talking about family or I'm finished. That's like half the book so far.

I know I KNOW. By the way, now that I have changed the title, I've got to go back and take out that line about the old title. It makes no sense now.

Remind me.

You might have noticed we have jumped all around. This is how my mind works. It is how memory works. At least my memory. I don't remember things in chronological order. I'm not sure I remember them in any order at all. This mind of mine, I'm lucky I remember at all.

Anyway, we will hop to my childhood. I mentioned it was not a fluffy cloud experience, but whose is? There were still good times. I'm sure there are funny things buried back there. Let us see.

I mentioned I do not lie well? This is not new. When I was six I kissed a boy for 50 cents. Well, he was not a boy, he was a teenager. He lived across from me. Anyway, I was a greedy six year old, 50 cents, a kiss on the cheek.

Naturally, my mother wanted to know where this windfall came from. I could tell from her tone that I had to come up with something fast.

I told her I found these two quarters in a crack in the snow. It was winter, this much was logical.

My mother, I told you, was not stupid. She did not believe me.

I recall she told the woman across the street to keep her little pervert away from me. Her words. Not mine. I do not know that he was a pervert. Last I heard he was not in jail or accused of horrible things.

There WAS a pervert in our neighborhood, not this boy. At least I was told he was. They didn't call them that then, they called them dirty old men. I stayed away, I was a good child. I think. Now these are tales I heard, about this man. He never landed in jail to the best of my knowledge either. Also, he was old.

My parents separated shortly before this memory. Dad was off somewhere doing Dad things. He was a wanderer. He wandered in and out of my life throughout my childhood.

Anyway, I was also adopted by half the neighborhood. The parents, I think they just spelled each other. A group of us played together, and so we were always at each others' houses. A normal thing I think.

Most mothers then were housewives. There were cookies. I liked the cookies. I liked their mothers. I liked their fathers, although fathers then, they stood back. I'm sure they played catch with their boys, all those father things. We were girls. Mainly the fathers told us to "Pipe down.", or "keep it to a dull roar."

I loved school. I read lots of books. I rode my bike. Kid things.

My mother worked. I never saw this as a bad thing. I didn't feel abandoned, I didn't feel she should be home baking cookies, this was just how it was. BROTHER is six years older than me, so when I was in elementary he was home roughly a half hour before me.

He was out at 2:30, I was out at 3:00 Mom was out at 4:00. It worked. For me and Mom, not so much for BROTHER, I suppose. It probably sucked having to baby-sit all the time.

I looked up to BROTHER, of course I did. I also loved him, hated him, thought him my hero, and thought him a jerk. All at different times of course. I wasn't crazy quite yet.

BROTHER was funny. He could make me laugh even just after he had made me cry. He still can for that matter. Make me laugh. It's been a long time since he's made me cry.

I was NOT funny. Not a bit. Everything was very serious to me. What to wear. What someone said on the playground. SERIOUS. BROTHER saw everything as funny, sooner or later. Perhaps over the years it has rubbed off on me, I don't know.

Mostly we got along. I was an irritating little sister, I'm quite sure, but there wasn't a WHOLE lot to argue about. After all, he was six years older. When I was 6, he was 12. That's like 100 years in kid time. Now it's nothing. A heartbeat, maybe two.

So there wasn't the fighting over the toys thing, with us. Unless I messed with his things. I don't remember doing this, but I'm sure I probably did. All little kids like stuff that isn't their stuff. It's much more interesting.

I jumped on the bed. Somehow I created a hole, a dent. That's where I slept, in the dent.

Right up until I broke the bed, jumping on it. Then it was a mattress on the floor for about a year. Maybe not that long, memory is funny.

At some point I was back in a bed, nice white headboard. We had a dog. Sandy. His name I can tell you. First he is a dog, second he's dead. He won't care.

Prattle On - Teri Stricker

Sandy was a MUTT. My mother got him when I was very small. He looked like an unclipped big poodle gone amok. His hair was the color of sand, That's where he got his name. I remember him leaping into the car that first day. I was worried he would land on me. He didn't.

My mother got him on a whim, I think. The reason I think this is because my father was very surprised to come home that night to a snarling barking dog. It woke us up. I was 4 or less, I think.

Anyway, it got sorted out and Sandy was my Dad's dog from the moment he decided Dad lived there. When the parents separated, he was BROTHER's dog.

This was a bone of contention with me. I wanted Sandy to be MY dog. I was the baby, I was supposed to get what I want, right? Sandy didn't agree. He slept with BROTHER. He only slept with me if BROTHER went on a sleepover.

Then I would complain too. Sandy took up the whole bed. He's on his side, paws out. Then he would stretch. THUMP! I am on the floor. There was no pleasing me, I tell you.

As a teenager, I still loved school, still loved books. Now I wrote horrible poems about how life sucked. At the time, I was sure my life was the worst on the planet. I know better now. I also know now my life, it wasn't so bad. All teenagers feel this way.

When I was fifteen it was Dad's turn to try and finish raising me. He was with my stepmother by then.

I was a cynical teenager. I had decided that people were only nice when they wanted something.

Stepmother was nice. I didn't trust her. But I could think of nothing she could want from me. Besides, of course, to get that teenage snarl off my face, I'm sure.

You know the look I am talking about. It's defiant. For no reason. No one has told you to do anything even. It just stays there. I don't know why. Maybe it is part of the face's development, I don't know.

Prattle On - Teri Stricker

Anyway, eventually I got to like and trust stepmother. She was no worse than any grownup as far as I could see.

Now I got to be Daddy's girl for a while again. This wasn't so bad. I remember long talks about nothing long after I should have been in bed. This was his farming period, so I learned how to milk a cow. Also goats.

I slopped hogs, I gathered eggs. I loved it. I didn't do this all myself, I was not the family slave. The chores were a family affair. I never felt that ho hum time to feed the chickens thing. Of course, it was all very novel at the time.

My father is very good with animals. Any animals. The cow, and the pigs, came when he called them. This is convenient when they break out of their pens let me tell you. The chickens even wanted to be petted.

We had a little rooster. I don't remember his name. He was a very proud little thing. Roosters have spurs on the back of their feet, I don't know if you know. His broke off, it bled.

I don't know how much you know about chickens, but they are not very nice to each other when one is hurt. They will peck at the wounded one and make it worse. So we have to fix it.

Dad does this. For one thing, he is the only one this rooster is going to sit still for, and for another he knows what he's doing. Well, I think.

So the leg is bandaged. This rooster strutted for a week or so with that bandage. It was a badge of honor or something. That, or he just appreciated not being pecked anymore.

The animals, they get out sometimes. It's a fact of life. My father was a drill machine operator in a factory, the farm was just, you know fun.

I would come home on the school bus, and sometimes I would have animals to greet me. My friends loved it. "There's Teri's family!"

This was good natured ribbing, not the horrible stuff kids do to each other earlier in life.

So I would get off the bus and lead them to their respective pens. Sometimes it was the cow. Sometimes the goats. Once or twice the pigs. I smile at the memory, and I don't recall getting upset then either. It was all good.

Dad and my stepmother were also secretly working on my confidence level during this time. It did improve. I changed schools when I moved in with them, for the first time in my school life I was not sitting next to the same people I had since kindergarten.

It was an adventure. I made friends. As I said somewhere back there in the chapters of drivel, I was joining the Navy soon. I also mentioned Dad was a wanderer.

They moved to Florida from Michigan when I was 17. They didn't wind up in Alaska, although my father probably wouldn't have minded. Just another wander. He was not a normal man. He consulted the map, he didn't just fold it.

I had the option of moving with them, but I didn't want to change schools for one semester.

So I moved back with my Mom. This wasn't bad. We'd had time to cool off after all the tussling and all that landed me at my father's in the first place, and I wasn't home much. First, this school counted credits differently so I had to pack that semester with credits to graduate in time.

Second, I babysat after school until sometime in the evening. It was my first job if you don't count the blueberry picking I did for a whole week before I quit at 13 or 14.

So we got along, I graduated. I was shown to the relatives and given money by some for food on my trip, or whatever they thought I needed.

No one thought I'd actually get through boot camp, including me. But I was making an effort. My mother cried seeing me off on the greyhound. I was touched. So I made my way into the world of ADULTHOOD. Well, sorta. Being in the military is kind of like having a safety net, but it was CLOSE to adulthood.

So see? I had a childhood. My children still don't believe it. My son used to ask me what it was like having a baby dinosaur as a pet. He found that very funny. Me, not so much.

And yes, you are right, thank you. It is time to chapter

Prattle On - Teri Stricker
Chapter Twenty Six - School

Ah, we are back from the bathroom, or dinner. Or perhaps we are settling into bed. Reading our drivel to put us to sleep. This is good, I don't mind. I've put more than one listener to sleep. It's a talent I have.

So let us wander out the front door to school. School is different things to different people. To some it is the football field, the soccer field, these active things.

To others it is where they met the person they married later in life. Sadly, in many cases, the FIRST spouse, but not the last.

But I digress. Again. Remember, we are driveling.

Anyway, we drive up. Most of us spent a lot of time here. For those who did the sports, the football, the cheerleading, the basketball, they spent more than others. Also the chess team, I imagine.

So we open the double doors and we go on. First is the smell. Wooden pencils and wooden pencil sawdust. I know the smells some of you remember, that's closer to the gym.

To the right is the front office. In my day this was not big. The first door takes you to the first desk, or window. It was a desk for me, or a bar, it was a tall thing, I remember that.

This is where you come if you are late. You tell your sad tale and you get your pass to get to class. Yes, I know, it rhymes. I am sorry. I did not mean to.

This is also where you come if you are in trouble. The principal is somewhere back there. Somewhere back there is also the permanent record they are always holding over our heads. There's a typewriter. Today, I know, it's a computer. This is my memory we are wandering, remember? So there is a typewriter. There are things on the walls telling us things, that we mostly ignore.

So, let us get our hall pass and move on out of here.

Across the lobby, we'll call it a lobby though it is really just a wide space, is the auditorium. This is another set of double doors. Open them, it's okay, we are invisible, we are adults, we will not get in trouble.

It's dark right now, but you can see the rows and rows of seats, you can see that there is a stage, some curtains. In my auditorium we had little desk arms to pull up. Assemblies are here, also study hall.

Today there is no study hall. No hour set aside for study. You take that home now, I guess. This could be because not a lot of studying actually got done there. Much whispering, giggling, and spitball throwing. Not much talking.

Let go the doors. Let them bang. I know, we shouldn't. Do it anyway. It makes a satisfying sound doesn't it?

Well we probably shouldn't go through the whole school. It is enough to see the lines of lockers, the artwork and all along the walls isn't it? Yes. Except I do want to visit a class.

So here, straight, then turn left down this hall. Now left, yes open that door, let us look in.

It is science class. Tables big enough for two students to sit at. There are beakers and test tubes and holders for the test tubes. Look, there I am. Wow, I look young. Walking across the floor. Quietly, oh so quietly. Mr. A does not like noise.

Mr. A. chews gum. You are not allowed to, however. He also fancies himself a comedian. So he shouts "Teri!" I with the tray of test tubes jump. Hell I in the doorway jump, he is still loud.

The test tubes go into the air. It is slow motion. They land, they break. The young Teri turns to face the mighty Mr. A. BROTHER has had this teacher, she has heard stories. She is scared out of her wits, but she doesn't look it, does she? I only know because it was me then.

She smiles a slow smile. It as not cocksure, like she thinks it is. She opens her mouth and says.

"What?"

He laughs. This is an odd sound, he is not known for this, at least not to this class. He only laughs at his own jokes. Come to think of it, this is his own joke. The answer, that was just a bonus.

"Clean that up."

There are many classes, many lockers. My favorite room in the whole world, the library. I read a lot of the books on those shelves. This is where I met Stephen King. Well not the man, the books he wrote. Carrie, Cujo, you know the ones I mean. Of course he's written many more since. I also met Thoreau and Shakespeare and the Bronte girls.

And if I list them all this will be 200 pages in no time, and really, do you care? Not so much. It is all here. On the way home from school is the public library, I haunted that one even more. It was open when I wasn't supposed to be in class.

My other favorite room is down here, by the back door. It's not much to look at. Auditorium style seats because they are layered. In front a Piano, a set of risers. This was the choir room. Here we made music, we sang wonderful songs. I was a first soprano. I am not now.

I was not overly accomplished, I wasn't in any of the special groups. This would make me stand out. I worked very hard at not standing out. Not just here. Anywhere. Fit in, that's all I wanted.

It was never going to happen, not really. Not until I was much older and much less serious. Hell, who am I kidding, I don't fit in NOW, I just don't care. But the music was a joy.

In high school I didn't get teased so much. Elementary, then junior high is where most of that happens. Maybe if I had tried to talk to folks once in high school, they might have talked back. I had friends, don't get me wrong. They were the other misfits. They would probably not tell you I was shy. I wasn't, when I was with them.

Anyway I don't tell you this to make you pity me. It is the past, after all. And kids tease. It's all in how you process it. I'm just explaining why these two rooms were the favorite.

I told you I came back to this school after I'd lived with my Dad for a time. I did talk more, and the classmates were friendly enough. I wasn't comfortable even then, but they talked. They were not cruel. I had been gone two years, and I was different, they were different, and maybe my absence made me interesting. I don't know.

I went to my 20 year reunion, when it was time to do that. Most of the folks I actually hung with were not there, we were the misfits after all. But these are people I saw every day for a lot of years, so we knew each other anyway.

I was like I am now, and I didn't suddenly freeze up and become a kid again. So I laughed, I joked, I visited. They were amazed. I guess I don't blame them. After all this is not who they grew up with. This me, this is who was hiding under the shy.

So it was a good night. If I had any grudges (I don't THINK I did.), they would have been gone after that, that is all I can tell you.

So I was not the homecoming queen. Only one girl per class can be that after all. I was not a cheerleader. This is a good thing, I was not terribly coordinated. I could have hurt myself.

I did play sports. I did. They yelled my name. "Teri! HOW could you miss that!?" Oh well.

It is time to chapter again. This seems to be happening faster, but it isn't really. Perhaps I immersed myself in this one. Come along now, we don't want to be tardy.

Prattle On - Teri Stricker
Chapter Twenty Seven – The Senses

So we are not tardy. This is good. I hate going to the office, don't you?

As I took that walk through the school, I realized memories are more than fragmented pictures that roam through your mind. They are. There are smells.

I'm not talking about THAT smell. THAT one is not fun. You know the one I mean. "What is that SMELL?" Yeah, that one.

You and your family trek through the house trying to track it down, and eventually (at least we hope so) you find it, and fix it.

But, no. I am discussing here the memory smells. The smells that take you back in time. The smell of newly mown grass. This works in two ways. One is, it usually takes you back to childhood, two is, it reminds you to mow YOUR grass.

The smell of Lilacs, this reminds me of my mother. That was her flower. We had a bush, and in early spring we picked some and brought them into the house. So her face is forever associated with lilacs to me.

The smell of hot tar. This reminds me of a summer the road crew came through and did all the roads in my neighborhood. The teenage girls often talked to them, flirted with them. This could be what made this job take all summer, I don't know.

The smell of Pollen. Yes, in high summer it has a smell. It's a strong smell. You smell it you remember playing baseball in that empty lot near your house maybe.

Houses have a smell. Again not THAT smell. Just a smell all their own. Your grandmother's house. Your favorite aunt's house.

YOUR house has a smell too, you just don't smell it. It is OUR smell.

Prattle On - Teri Stricker

People have smells. It is why when your husband is gone on a trip, you use his pillow. It's comforting.

Dogs know this. They know us by our smell. Our smell is how they get to know us. They smell us coming from a mile away.

Children know smell. Nana has a smell, Papa, he has another smell. We sweat, well then the smell is too much and we should shower.

I moved back to the neighborhood I grew up in for a while after my mother died. When I went to visit the neighbors I'd grown up knowing, the first thing, is you walk in the house.

The smell of said house, takes you back. Sometimes it takes us to a particular day, usually not. Suddenly you are young again, for a few minutes. It's not so bad, unless of course your not so fluffy cloud memories are really bad and you like, saw a murder in this house or something. Then I suppose, this would be not so good.

So smell is big for us. Not so much as for a dog, but we do use it.

Luckily we also have this thing called selective perception. Unlike dogs, we are discerning folks. Some things smell just plain awful. A skunk that just sprayed in the area, things like this. The chicken coop.

Then our mind lets us get used to this smell, and we are not smelling it anymore. This comes in handy. Especially if you are cleaning the chicken coop.

Our noses tell us when dinner is cooking. They also tell us when dinner is burning, before the smoke gets thick and we have to open all the doors and windows.

I am a smoker. I think I said. So my nose, it's not so sensitive. Hunts for THAT smell, I need another family member to help. If it is a strong smell I smell it, but I guess I have less Beagle in me for the tracking down part than the rest of the family.

Prattle On - Teri Stricker

You know when the laundry is washing by the smell. You don't have to hear the washer, the smell drifts up to the rest of the house and you say someone is doing laundry.

The heat in your house. After the first few times, of the season, we don't smell the furnace heating our home anymore, but it didn't go anywhere. We just don't smell it anymore. Not consciously anyway.

The smell of baby powder maybe reminds you when your children were little. It brings a smile.

That new doll smell. Okay, sorry guys, you don't know this one so much, maybe. Ask your wife, she'll know exactly what I am talking about.

So, smell is good.

Sounds evoke memories too. The first sound to come to mind is the music of course. You hear a song, it takes you back. You may even remember where you heard it first, but other times, it's just a feeling.

Think, for example of the sounds of summer. Kids laughing, screaming, and carrying on somewhere down the road. Screen doors slamming. Music drifting up the street or out of a car's windows as it passes.

If you live by the beach, it has sounds. Splashing, the kids playing again, boat motors.

Places change what they look like over the years. New houses go up, old ones come down, people remodel.

The sounds don't. Many of the smells don't. So you go back to your hometown 20 years later, and there's a mix.

The sounds and the smells take you back, but you are looking and there are things you never saw before. So your mind is kind of confused.

The sound of a small child's laugh. Enjoy it. It is the epitome of happiness. It bubbles out of them, doesn't it? They couldn't contain it if they tried. It's beautiful.

Prattle On - Teri Stricker

We used to laugh like that, you and I. What happened? Life. We have the bills and the children we have to buy the clothes for. We have the idiots we have to deal with at the office. These things. Oh, sometimes something deliciously funny will trigger a laugh like that from us, still. It's rarer though, we must admit it.

Sometimes we have to stop that child's laughter, like when they are climbing the dressers. We have to come in the room and say "get down." This is life.

Besides this, if we don't stop them, they will stop when the dresser lands on top of them. Then maybe there's the trip to the ER because they broke something. So go ahead, tell them to get down. They will laugh again in ten minutes, I assure you.

This child's laugh thing, even if you are trying to sleep it is beautiful. You want to get upset with them, but really, it is too wonderful a laugh. You still tell them to "Pipe down!" because we are parents, that is our job. But you are smiling. Good thing they can't see us smiling in the dark of our room, they'd never shut up.

Smiling in the dark is a good time to chapter, don't you think. Yes. Me too. Let us do it.

Chapter Twenty Eight – Digressing About Everything

Morning has broken. Got a screwdriver? I never understood that phrase. What is broken? The sun and the moon are doing exactly what they are supposed to do.

Somewhere, in the country, roosters crow. They greet the day.

In town people are getting up, and getting ready for work. Some are whistling, some are scowling.

There are people who get up well, and people who do not. My husband, he bounces up and seizes the day.

Me, I slowly get up, and I kind of PAT the day. I come out and everything is blurry for a few minutes, and very bright.

I stumble outside to freeze for the morning cigarette, then stumble to the coffee maker. Somewhere in the midst of the first cup of coffee, I am awake.

I don't like to talk in the morning, during the stumble phase.

I realize this is difficult to believe. You've noticed that as a rule, talking I like. True. Just not when I first get up.

My GIRL, she is more stumbly than I am. She comes out of the bedroom with this look. She is not quite awake, it is obvious, and she's not terribly happy about how awake she already is, this is the look I speak of.

Don't talk to her. Don't do it, she will bite your head off. I don't bite your head off I just sit quietly and let it wash over me. I just don't want to think about ANSWERING anything that early.

Some mornings my husband, who has seized the day an hour ago is right there. Asking questions. "Did this customer pay?"

"I don't know. You see my computer out here on the patio?"

Prattle On - Teri Stricker

He sighs. I don't blame him, but don't make me think before I've been up 5 minutes.

Any time of day, I take people as they are. That sounds simple. I know. But people always want to change other people, I've noticed.

Especially people we love. You can't. Stop it.

I have a friend. She is a stress queen. She just is. I try to help her by making her laugh, this relaxes her a bit for a few minutes, but, I can't make her suddenly not be a stress queen. It's in her make up, it is what she is.

Another friend, he takes forever to answer you. This is how he is. He's not ignoring you, he's thinking. A lot. Eventually he will answer.

The worst is in love. I don't understand it. You fell for this person they ARE. Now you want they should change everything about themselves so they fit this picture in your head.

Stop it. It won't happen. Either take them as they are or, move on. They may WANT to mold themselves to your expectations, they can't do it.

Say you are 30. That's 30 years of being you. 30 years of events, feelings, relationships, have MADE you who you are. Now comes this guy or girl. They love you, you love them. YAY! Now they want you to change – EVERYTHING.. HUH?

I don't know about you, I am not a doll. There is also no string to pull to make me talk, with several things in there to say.

I think something, I say it. That is me. If you don't like talking to me, well then you don't like me. Move on. There are millions of other people. One of those others might live up to your standards. One boyfriend he thought I should use smaller words. He claimed HE understood me, but others wouldn't.

Prattle On - Teri Stricker

I hadn't noticed this problem. I bought him a dictionary, I moved on. I wasn't using words like "euphonious" or anything. I was talking much like I am typing to you. Like I talk.

At ten years old I did use the ten dollar words. Made me feel smart. For a short time. Then you realize that since no one has a clue what you are saying, there is no conversation, only yourself spouting words and them, looking confused. I stopped.

My best trait AND my worst trait, is I am adaptable. If I am talking to you, and you to me, suddenly, your words become my words. Some I keep. My husband hates this. Like the word ain't. He doesn't like that word. I use it. Poor thing, he'll get over it.

"It's not a WORD!!!!" he'd say. I'd say "Yep, it is. It's in the dictionary now." That isn't his point. I am sorry.

Perhaps this goes back to the child who wanted to fit in, I don't know. I mean, I don't repeat your sentences back to you or anything. For instance this friend online used to say and stuff. A lot. I picked it up. I didn't steal it. It rubbed off. Or, "you know".

My daughter says "whatever" a lot, for example. I hate it. Then I catch myself SAYING it. I growl.

I don't cuss overly much, those words I do my best NOT to pick up. And I DO ask people not to use that "F" word. I know, changing people, shame on me. But often there are children near.

It is also short term, you can go home and "F" all you want. Just, not in front of my grandchildren. This is a respect thing, that's all.

I am fond of adjectives. Believe it or not, the "F" word, it's not an adjective. I mean we could take the word "aid", and do the same thing.

"That aiding idiot crashed my aiding car into an aiding tree!!!"

Doesn't sound right, does it? I know. The only reason that the "F" word sounds right, is because you hear it ALL THE TIME.

I was a sailor, I cussed like one. I am not better than you. I don't pretend to be. It's not about better. I had "effing" issues, ok? I got out of the Navy and slowly got rid of that vocabulary. You pick it up, whether you are fond of it or not, hearing it all the time, that's all.

I had small children. Your mother, she looks at you funny if her grandchild asks her to pass the "effing" peas, you see what I'm saying?

This is no different, to me, than not going to Walmart naked. It's a social thing. Or that torturous custom of shaving the legs.

But asking you to suddenly be someone else 24 hours a day to make this person happy, this is different. You want me to dress different, walk different, speak differently, everything.

Online, I meet people from all over the globe. You are talking in text, you are not encumbered with how they look. You can also talk using your microphone, but then the accents may hinder conversation.

I have a Southern US accent. They may have an Italian, Argentinean, or German accent. You get the idea. In text, the words might be in the wrong order, we parse our sentences differently than most other languages, but you can figure out what they are saying.

This tells me a bit about people, that maybe if you haven't mixed like this, you don't know. We are all people. Language barriers aside. I am as interested in where they live as they are about where I live.

They know much more about my country than I know about theirs. Even considering the language barrier, their education level is better than most Americans I meet. Why is this? I don't know.

There is much I have learned that has surprised me. For example in the UK they don't have refrigerators with icemakers and water in the door. My UK friend that I mentioned this to was astounded by this idea.

We eat differently, we consider different things important sometimes. But we are all people. Obviously I would know more about all of this if I actually got on a plane and went over there. Walked around. However, this is expensive. I still learn more talking to people than I do from the books.

There are the jerks, no matter where you tread, out in the world we live in, or ONLINE. We ignore them. They go away. The jerks hail from every country. No one country has the patent on jerks I assure you.

In one program, Second Life, the one I sing in, they have little translator programs. You wear them. This makes conversation easier, you type in your language, they type in theirs.

However, these translators are not perfect. So you may see some FUNNY sentences, and so may they. You may say, "I am drinking" the translator may tell them "I am a frog." This sort of thing. We all know it. We giggle, we go on.

We've come to the end of another long ramble of mine. I have no idea how I got from morning to International conversations. I just read it, I still do not know. This must be why it is drivel, right?

In any case, we should chapter before I ramble on even more. We like our chapters.

Chapter Twenty-Nine - Moods

My cat is meowing. He wants me to feed him, because he can see that centimeter at the bottom of his bowl. I am talking to him.

"I am NOT giving you more food until you finish it. We have plenty, but we will not waste. And WHY am I talking to a cat."

We do it though, don't we? The cat is understandable, he responds to the rhythms of our voices, he understands his name, these things.

We also talk to the computer when it is not doing what we like, however. This machine understands nothing. It only SEEMS like it is laughing at us.

I yell at the desk if I have gotten up and bumped my knee. The desk does not care. It doesn't even know I slipped and said a bad word.

We impart personality to inanimate objects. I do it. You do it. Come now, admit it.

We are not always reasonable when we hurt ourselves either. For instance DAD. If you trip over something he left in the middle of the room, well you should have looked where you are going. This is true.

If HE trips over something YOU have left in the middle of the room, "Why is this HERE! It does not BELONG here!" This is also true.

However, if it does not belong there when I leave it, neither does it when HE leaves it there, correct? Correct. So we are not reasonable when in pain. This is understandable.

Anger is not reasonable, and NEITHER is love. There is a reason you've heard people say "I love that person beyond all reason." Emotion knows no reason.

Do I have an example? Of course I do, what do you take me for? I laugh.

Prattle On - Teri Stricker

My mother and father had a fight one night. An argument. My mother was drunk AND angry, not the best combination.

My father, he was sober, and just wanted to finish watching the news, or whatever it was he was watching.

So she is yelling and being loud, he cannot hear the news. He picks her up, puts her out in the yard, goes in the house, closes the door.

Now, she is really mad. She storms to the door and pounds on it. He ignores her, and turns up the TV.

So, she threw her beer through the window of the door. My father gets up. Opens the door. He hadn't locked it.

In her anger, she assumed she locked it.

He said, in that deadpan voice we have all heard when we have done something stupid, "Did it ever occur to you to turn the knob?"

No, it did not. She had two strikes against thinking, the anger and the being drunk. You see? An example.

I actually don't remember this, I remember the story. It was told by both parents, with a laugh, in my mother's case, with a rueful laugh. So I was probably not home for this.

So, emotion doesn't reason. Nor does alcohol.

Nor do I, apparently. My next sentence I was going to type was. "So think about this next time you get mad."

That won't work. You can't think. Oh well, DAD is the genius not me.

I get angry rarely. I don't know if this is because my parents were such emotional people who let it all hang out, or because I want to always be in control of myself, or maybe even because I automatically analyze everything.

Most of the time, I get mad, I walk away. DAD hates this, but he knows it will happen. I will be back later and discuss it calmly. I will not talk when I am angry. I also don't stay angry long. It is just not how I am.

This is not to say I give a cold shoulder. This is not a calculated effort.

The good news is, we don't argue much anyway. Usually something makes us mad, we blow off steam. You know. "You left the damn phone off the charger again!"

That's it. Not even an argument, it's over. No big thing. And even that is rare. We cruise along life together nicely. We've had a lot of practice.

Plus we are rarely in the same mood. He has a bad day, I either leave him alone or I cheer him up. The same vice versa.

Sometimes you want to be cranky. You don't WANT to be cheered up. This is just human. We all have those days.

Stress makes us cranky. I had one day I was dealing with a multitude of computer problems, this is my job. Every 5 minutes, DAD is asking for status, and SLSIL seems to be asking questions every 5 minutes too, but not the SAME 5 minutes. So I am getting maybe 2.5 minutes to THINK of the problem I am trying to solve; and then I am interrupted.

GIRL comes in. She has a simple unrelated question. She stands there, waiting. This is an interruption in itself. She has not been to my office, she has no idea what has been going on. It isn't her job to research what my day is like, after all.

I look up. "WHAT?! FOR PITY'S SAKE WHAT THE HELL DO YOU WANT?"

Like I say, I don't do this often. Poor GIRL is flabbergasted and a little scared, I guess. She actually backs away from me. "I'll ask later."

I apologized later. It is rare enough it merited her reaction, you see.

Was I reasonable? Of course not. I was frustrated. She just happened to be the one to be waiting there when I blew.

I just yell though. There's no flying missiles, no door slamming. You remember slamming the door as a child?

Open and close it 50 times, the right way.

I should have done that with my daughter. She slams.

All these pages to say emotion is unreasonable. I do like to talk, don't I? So, when your spouse is having a bad day, think about it before you talk to them. They will not be reasonable until they get it out of their system. Don't expect them to. Then if you go into the room with this expectation, you are not going to get your feelings hurt. See?

Have I beat this subject to death? Yes, probably. But then, every subject I've taken on, I've done the same thing. I don't know why you are reading this nonsense. I'm glad you are though!

So we Chapter and try to think of the next subject to beat to death.

Prattle On - Teri Stricker
Chapter Thirty – I Was Going To Have A Subject

Many people want beautiful lush, green grass. Some nice hedges. The hedges, they can usually work. The grass, rarely.

My yard has some grass. A rainbow of colors between lush green and dead brown. There are also lots of weeds, and crabgrass. I don't have the patience for it all. And there's the water bill. Besides, you water it, it grows, you have to mow it. Of course, you don't water it, it rains, you have to mow it.

I should just pave the whole yard. Then you just sweep. All nice and tidy, no mowing.

Some of us have gardens. DAD has a garden most years. He plants it. He goes out and does the miracle grow once a week, or whatever it is.

I water it daily. I weed. I keep the kids away from it. I lead him out and point out what is growing. He smiles.

But it is DAD's garden. I just get to do all the work. This is marriage. When things ripen then I lead him out and we pick.

DAD is the cook, the chef. He is good at it, I don't know why I am not very fat. He washes the dishes. He's not lazy, it's just the garden thing.

When we first got married, I stayed home with the kids for a while. About a year. I made menus. No, I kid you not, I really did. We shopped by my menus. I made Lasagna and Stroganoff and fancy things. I baked. We rarely had simple things like Spaghetti.

Then I went to work. I couldn't take all that domesticity. Plus we needed the money. So now we are coming home from work at the same time. I start to cook, he is there with input. "Why not add a little thyme?"

Cooking is work for me. You need to eat, so you cook. I didn't mind his input. But I started realizing that he ENJOYED it. On Saturday he would let me sleep in he would make a breakfast of champions.

Prattle On - Teri Stricker

I am sure he thought he would insult me by asking to cook. It was not that he didn't like what I cooked, but we are newlyweds after all, he didn't know how I might react. Also we are still in our twenties, and my hormones might still be raging, and are on occasion.

In those days I could weep despairingly over burnt cookies.

So finally, I said to him. "You like to cook, don't you?"

He nodded. That's what you do when you agree, I think.

I said, "So why aren't you? It's just another chore to me, and you like it. So cook."

This is not to say I never cook. I do. I am responsible for the pot roast and the fried potatoes. On the days that he doesn't want to cook, I can do so. I didn't forget how to follow a recipe, or anything. Although mostly, if he doesn't want to cook, there are plenty of leftovers to heat up.

Most of the chores fell out like that. Mostly there was no discussion about them. He likes the kitchen, so he does the kitchen. I do the laundry and the bathrooms, we both share in the rest of the house.

He irons. He never liked how I ironed. I don't know, maybe my creases aren't so good, or something. So he irons.

It works. I can't complain.

I hear men can't hit the hamper, but he mostly does. We all miss sometimes, even the women. That doesn't stop me from joking about it though. My husband being basically neat is not funny. So while I am finding a song at a gig, I will say.

"Why is it that a man can go play basketball, make 15 baskets in a row. Then he comes home, misses the hamper, misses the garbage, misses the TOILET for pity's sake?"

The women laugh. The men laugh ruefully; some of them. But this is not always true, of course. Some men CAN hit the hamper, the garbage, and all of this. They are the exception.

So I have an exceptional husband. This is a good thing. I can brag.

We don't talk constantly. He works. I work. He plays the piano, I sing. We feel we need a hug or to see that the other is alive, we go into their space. He often comes out and rubs my shoulders, I often wander into his area and kiss him. It works, what can I say?

Now when you have a house full of people, it is very hard to be spontaneously romantic. Someone is always wanting one of you for something. We are old, so even to GIRL and SLSIL, it never occurs to them we might do something in the bedroom besides fold laundry.

The closed door SHOULD be a clue. It is not. Maybe next time I'll hang a tie on it.

Then there are the grandchildren. The tie would not help, after all. They are 3 and 5 after all. They adore their Papa.

Knock knock. "Papa are you a'seepun?"

Oh dear. They've learned to knock, but not to go away. So a moment later;

Knock Knock "Papa I really NEED you!"

So much for the romantic interlude. We smile, though. Night comes sooner or later after all.

And children are precious. They are. PAPA doesn't always think I know it. I do. I just get irritated.

When GIRL works, I baby sit. Even with my sense of humor I do not LITERALLY sit on them, although at times, it is a tempting thought.

We draw. We play roll the ball. We color. I play silly stuff on the computer, and they draw, color, or roll the ball. Until the ball leaves the floor.

Then we take the ball away. Most days, this is not a problem. Some days they are monsters. Children can be like that. I had my grandson in time out 20 times in one day, once. He is stubborn. This might be because I don't leave him there long though.

Children are loud. God made them this way. We say "pipe down!" a lot.

It is not all work. We go outside, I show them the snails and the worms hiding under the rocks. We point at lizards, they chase the butterflies.

Showing a child something new, like the day we found a snake, is exhilarating. They are so excited. It excites you. It was the same when mine were children of course, but this was 20 years ago, you understand.

For these precious people, we keep the grass. We mow. Well, actually SLSIL mows, but the point is it gets mowed. Imagine that, we came back to the beginning at the grass mowing. How did I do that? No clue.

Well since we have closed a circle, as it were, it must be time to chapter. You think?

Yes.

Chapter Thirty One - Children

We keep coming back to family and home, because this is a huge part of life. There are other things. Music, art, a good restaurant. It's true, they exist.

As I said, I sing. ONLINE. I am not on a camera when I do this, so I don't have to put on the makeup and the fancy clothes. I don't even have to shave my legs if I don't want to, that I do for DAD.

Music is a huge part of my life, even without singing. Everything I do, I can match a song to it. This is weird, but true. I burst into song in the middle of the kitchen if there is a phrase that I hear that is in a song.

The family is used to this. They don't run screaming from the room, they don't call the white coats, they just smile. I'm harmless, after all.

So while my children grew, music was there. DAD plays the keys, I sing, and the kids were surrounded by it. They love music. GIRL likes to sing as she does her chores and listens to music a lot.

BOY sings too, if he thinks no one is listening, but mostly he just likes to hear good music. Of course, we don't always agree on what is good.

As a teenager he liked RAP. I said I would have none of that crap blaring on my stereo, and no RAP CDs would come into my house.

Then I heard Will Smith. He wasn't doing the cussing and the sex and the beating of women in his raps, so I got BOY one of his CDs.

BOY and I both love the Dr. Demento series and Ray Stevens, and Weird Al, the funny stuff.

So I had things in common with both children besides the fact that I brought them into the world and we all sat at the same table for dinner.

Prattle On - Teri Stricker

I adore my children, I adore my grandchildren. I was never really into OTHER kids. I had nothing against them, I didn't sharpen my axe, waiting for them to come into my house or anything, I just didn't think much about them at all.

But eventually my children got old enough to go outside and play in the neighborhood. And naturally, they played with other kids. Good kids, mostly. So these kids would wander in behind my kids.

Some were the children of people I grew up with. Some were not. The kids all loved their bikes and to play ball, and outdoor things, so mostly they were outside.

This was good.

In the meantime, I have a friend. Her parents and my parents knew each other when they were young. At one time we were probably playing on the same blanket. However, that is before either of our memories begins.

She lived in the same town, within walking distance to my house, but not in my neighborhood. We were in the same grade.

For years she hated me. I either don't remember why or she never told me. It doesn't matter, anyway. But about age 12 we became friends. I should give her a name. Let's call her GIGI. Her name is absolutely nothing like GIGI, I just like the name. Anyway, let us go on.

We have always had an odd relationship, at least the grown up one. We don't hug when we see each other after a long time. We both grew up in hug-free zones. We love each other. I would say she was like a sister, except we have never fought, or argued. We are a lot alike in many ways. I came back from the Navy, we picked up as if we were in the middle of a conversation and one just went to the bathroom. It's nice, a friend like that.

GIGI is a very good artist. I won't gush, I'm not good at it, but she's good. At the time period we are in, she was teaching me to draw. She did a great job, I did not.

But as I was dabbling in the arts, I had the charcoal, and the pastels, the pencils and the sharpeners. The toys of the trade, in other words. I even tried painting.

So now comes Halloween. I'd learned several Halloweens before that the makeup you buy for costumes doesn't let the skin breathe. GIRL was the guinea pig, and she broke out in a rash.

So up to this year we'd done very little in the makeup department.

BOY wanted to be a vampire. So I floured his face, the lipstick and the eye liner.. and then I used a black pastel to do the circles under his eyes.

His friends loved it. Before I knew it I was creating Zombies in my kitchen. They went with one of the neighborhood mothers, and they had much fun. I stayed home with DAD and we passed out the candy and played spooky tapes. So we had fun too.

As they got older, somehow my house was the hangout for a lot of the kids. I don't know why. I was mean. I had one young man tell me. "You can't tell me what to do. You can't spank me or anything"

I said calmly. "I can tell you to go home. This is my home, and I have rules."

I never had another problem with him.

I was not overly nice, I didn't join in their conversations, at least most of the time, so I was mystified by the whole thing. Some even called me "Mom"

Very odd. So I ask BOY how this could be.

"You don't talk down to them. They like that."

Oh. I don't know why I would want to talk down to them. I never did to my children, even when they were little. I didn't use that irritating sweet googly voice when I talked to them either, well, not after they were up on their feet, anyway. I might have used it when we were playing silly games or tickling, I don't recall.

Anyway, kids are smart. You have to explain things sometimes, of course you do, they are not born knowing everything. But I have to explain things to people all the time when I fix their computers. I don't talk down to them either. One is a contractor. He's obviously smart, he just doesn't know computers. He can build a house. I can't. We are equal. Easy.

So, in a nutshell that was all it was. I treated them like people. Wow. I'm sure their parents must have too, I mean what else do you treat your children like, poodles?

When I was a kid, we had a hangout and called one mother Mom as well. I think maybe for the same reason? I don't know it was a very long time ago.

So, don't talk down to the kids. You can talk down to the dog, he doesn't care.

Yes, I think so, it is time to chapter.

Prattle On - Teri Stricker

Chapter Thirty Two – Jealousy And Peer Pressure

So we are driveling along here, aren't we? Well I am, you are reading. I should try to remember that.

You poor thing.

So, let's talk about jealousy. That green-eyed little devil. You have met him.

Most people think of jealousy to do with man and woman. This is not always true. Think back to your childhood. Friends got jealous if you spent the day with another friend. The problem is, some don't grow out of this.

I don't understand it. It is very odd, this jealousy. Now, if my husband went looking for the greener grass, of course I would be upset. This is normal.

But, people don't wait for things to actually happen. They act jealous for no reason at all.

You say hi to the mailman, and this person is suddenly sure you are sleeping with him. I don't understand. I have never had this problem with DAD, just so you know. DAD is smart, I told you.

But, how do you sleep with the mailman? There's one seat. Not a very big one either. He's at your door a minute. Mostly less.

And in the back is all the mail. It's also not very private, a mail truck.

So you go to Walmart, you talk to the clerk. Now you are sleeping with him. I don't know how this happens. The jealous mind eludes me. I do know it is irritating, this jealousy.

I had a jealous boyfriend once. No reason. This did not last long, because again, this is irritating. They want to beat up everyone you talk to, for one thing. It's hard to have a conversation with someone when your boyfriend is looking daggers at them.

Prattle On - Teri Stricker

I am not gorgeous. I never WAS gorgeous. I am mildly attractive. So are most people. So how this particular boyfriend thought everyone wanted my body, I don't know. He didn't even get my body, so why would he think anyone else would?

Emotion doesn't reason. I think I said.

Any time you are not with them, they dream up scenarios in their heads. We were minors. Usually I was not with him I was either with my parents or in a classroom. Yet he would find things I could have done.

Like I said, this did not last long. Irritating.

It's flattering for maybe ten minutes, this thinking you are all that, so that the world wants you Then it is old. It happens fast.

Most "going steady" lasts about a month when you are 14. This was a week. The rest of the month was telling him to go away. Go far away, find someone else to irritate.

I hope he got some confidence or something as he grew up.

This is not limited to men. Women are no better. They go through the pockets, they ask things like "Is her ass nicer than mine?"

Men look at women. This is a fact of life. They do it. They are often not so good at hiding it. They are men. I told you men and women are different. Though in this case, not always so much. Women ogle men too these days, and some are no more discreet than the men.

If this person is with you, generally, this is because they want to be. Unless you have a gun to their head, they can leave at any time.

Of course, people do cheat. It happens. But you know, wait for it to happen. Don't borrow trouble. Yes this is one of those THEY SAYs isn't it? It's a true one. Enjoy today. Not everyone is a skirt chaser or a man chaser.

Then there are the friends. You go to another friend's house for the day, they are hurt. WHY? They have other friends, you are not their only friend in the world. But you are supposed to sit around and wait for them to have time for you. I'm not so good at waiting. I like to talk. Laugh. And stuff.

So stop it. It's stupid, it makes no sense.

I wasn't a follower as a kid, but I was also not a leader. In school, I was a misfit, but in my neighborhood I had friends. There was a group of us girls, we hung out.

That's what you do as a teenager in a small town, you hang out. Not much else to do. You talk, you do each others' hair, and you hang out. Most of the talk is about boys, school, how horrible your parents are.

All parents are horrible. It's our job, isn't it. We have to give our kids something to talk about, after all.

Anyway, you also talk about what to do, rather than hang around. Some ideas are maybe not so good.

Once they wanted to go throw apples at cars. I don't know why. I thought of my horrible mother and what would happen if I got caught throwing apples at cars. I said;

"Well, have fun, I think it's time to go home anyway."

There were parties. One of the reasons my mother was horrible is I had a curfew. It was earlier than my friends' curfews. I didn't mind so much when there were these parties. They got old.

Somehow someone gets beer. So next you find a place to party. Usually a wide spot in the woods.

I wanted to fit in so I have a beer. I don't like beer. So I walk around the whole time with the same beer. From time to time I find a spot to pour a little out. I fit in this way. But my mother won't smell beer on my breath.

Except she already has beer on HER breath, she might not smell it.

Since I don't like beer anyway, this is not a problem. Except somehow, I've found, at parties, you wind up smelling like beer. People get drunk and they spill it. Some very original person, also drunk, yells out "alcohol abuse!."

How these people got home and went to bed and all without their parents knowing they were drunk I don't know. They did it, that's all I DO know.

So I was not a very exciting kid. No long talks with a police officer, no staggering into the house trying to pretend I'm sober. I was a good kid. I don't know if I was good because I was smart, or because I was terrified of my mother. Whatever it was, it worked, you see.

So jealousy and parties. No, I don't know how one led to another either. We should probably chapter before it leads somewhere else yet again. Come on, it could be fun. No apples, though, put them down.

Prattle On - Teri Stricker
Chapter Thirty Three – SPAM – Not The Edible Kind

Chain letters. They were bad enough in the mailbox. Now we have ONLINE. E-Mail. Why do people fall for this? Do they REALLY think if they send this E-Mail to 3000 people Bill Gates will give them money?

If they do believe this WHY? Why would Microsoft give money to people for cluttering up the Internet with trash? The mayor of your town, he doesn't pay you for dumping your junk on the highway, why should Microsoft? I don't know, I'm just asking.

This is why there is a delete key on the keyboard. Then there are the pray for this person you don't know and send it to 1000 people chain letters. Nice thought. 2 of those 1000 people might read it, you don't know. Perhaps I don't have a strong enough faith in prayer, or I'm lazy. But I don't send them.

Now then, we have the reason we have to send these chain letters, this is the same as the ones you got in the mail sometimes.

"If you send this to seven people you will have good luck for seven days." What a nice thought.

If you don't send it, oh my, you are in real trouble.

"Your horse will keel over, land on your pig, and both will die."

This one is not so bad, I don't have a horse OR a pig. We move on.

"Your husband will catch you with your boyfriend."

I don't have a boyfriend. So far I am safe.

"You will catch a fatal disease and by this time this month you will be dead."

Ouch. Maybe I should send it? No. So far I am dead 35 times. It's not so bad.

Then there is the spam. Okay, well the OTHER spam. This is stuff from people you never met, don't want to meet, and from E-mail addresses you couldn't reply to if you wanted to.

If it happens to be a real address it really still doesn't matter because either Hotmail (or whoever it is) has a limit on just how many messages your inbox can hold. And by 2AM there are already 2000 OTHER emails telling them to go jump in the lake

VIAGRA this is a big one. I get at least 50 a day for this. I guess it is not selling so well? You might have gotten the idea I am a man. I'm not. This won't work for me.

The other thing about VIAGRA is sometimes there is a reason you can't maybe get so excited. Your heart. Okay, let us get it out of our systems guys;

"OH BUT WHAT A WAY TO GO!!"

Maybe for you. Usually there is a partner involved. You maybe croaking on top of her could be traumatic you know. Even hookers have feelings after all.

Then the other warnings. "If you have an erection for more than four hours go to your doctor."

LORD help me four HOURS? This must be very tiring. Not only that, but now there is no blood going to your brain for that long. How do vegetables go to the doctor?

And how embarrassing is this, anyway? "UH, Doc, I have this problem."

"So I see."

No thanks.

The next 50 is stuff to make it bigger. I STILL don't have one, this doesn't matter.

Then there are the meet singles. These should have been first, no? I mean, why do you need VIAGRA or to make it bigger if there is no one to play with? Yeah, I don't know either.

Then there is money. I like money.

MAKE MONEY FAST! I'd love to. Really, I would, but these take you to a site where you pay them to tell you how. THEY are making money fast. I am too honest to.

These spammers like to pretend they are nice, and so you read. (if you are silly enough to open this E-mail rather than use that handy delete key)

"Hi, you are receiving this solicitation because you had previously agreed to receive correspondence from us or one of our partners. If this service should fail to meet your expectations, feel free to disassociate yourself from our service." You do this by clicking HERE.

I DID? When? I don't remember this. How many partners do you have? Do you know that multiple partners is how you spread disease? Obviously not.

I am not positive, but I think what clicking HERE really does, is tells them they hit the jackpot. This address has a real person behind it. Now they sell it to more of these PARTNERS. So I never click HERE. I delete.

This is maybe a boring chapter if you are not ONLINE. I am sorry. Half the known universe is ONLINE, and has at least one e-mail address, so I'm trying to cover the bases.

But the regular mail has these things too. Everyone wants to give me a credit card. I am PRE-APPROVED.

So why the form? Just send me the card. I am approved, after all.

They all start "Dear Mr. Stricker."

So I give it to DAD. They obviously got the name wrong, I am not Mr. Stricker. DAD deposits it in the garbage and reassures me I do not look like a man.

Thank goodness. I was worried for a moment.

Also in the mail are the bills. Little pieces of paper with big numbers on them. I am not fond of these, but ignoring them gets my lights turned off. Also my ONLINE.

Speaking of which I paid my electric bill. I paid it ONLINE. This is convenient. Now I have a shut-off notice. $10.34. Interesting. I paid the exact number their very own web site gave me, and now I owe more on the same bill. Not the new, this is much more, you understand. They have my E-mail, they sent me a receipt. So now they spent money to REMIND me I owed something I didn't owe before.

Interesting.

$10.34, this is not so much. But. I went back and looked. I didn't mistype. I paid it a day late. Their own system told me what to pay, I paid it. Now they add the late fee. I've owed this 3 days, and I get a shut-off notice. Nice, huh? These people have my telephone, address, they have my email address, the receipt was emailed to me, after all.

So these things irritate me.

I digressed again, huh? Sorry. It must be time to chapter by now anyway.

Chapter Thirty Four – Searching For The Topic to Digress From

So I don't send chain letters, I get this SPAM, and I pay my bills. Now you know as much as I do.

Sometimes I am at a loss for a topic. So I Google. Google is a search engine, ONLINE. This can be funny in itself.

For example I search for Funny Topics. Because I want to make you laugh. I want you to laugh like a child, I want it to be an irrepressible laugh.

So I click to a site – "How to Come up With Funny Conversation Topics"

This looks promising. They mostly tell me what I already know. Most of this book is me looking back at things that I find funny, which is their first advice. So now there are other things I can click;

How to Converse with a Guy Online

How to Be Funny

How to Be Naturally Funny

How to Draw a Funny Looking Face

How to Take a Funny School Picture

Pasting from these sites is irritating, because it changes my font. This is the typeface, what the text looks like. Hold on I will fix it.

There, now we are back to normal. For me, anyway.

So first we have the first one. Now, how to talk to a guy online, I think the same way you talk to one offline. That's my theory, and what I do. I don't really talk to guys differently than I talk to girls, since I am not hunting Online Nookie. So we move on.

How to be funny. Maybe I should click this. I'm not doing such a great job? I will do this after this chapter I think.

THIS is the one I pasted it for. HOW TO BE NATURALLY FUNNY. Hmmm. I'm thinking if you are LEARNING this it is not so natural. I mean either you see funny in things, or you don't, right? This is why we have comedians, to show us the funny.

No, I'm not a comedian, though I do see the funny. I just laugh a lot.

I should acknowledge where this comes from. Though they might not exist by the time you read this. It doesn't matter. If it does, then you can go there and see for yourself.

http://www.wikihow.com/Come-up-With-Funny-Conversation-Topics. They have some good advice, it looks like, it just struck me funny, that naturally funny thing.

So I move to another site, since I am pretending I am already naturally funny. The next one, it doesn't thrill me. Every funny topic has been done, I know this. Including those I have covered in this book of drivel. It is just that some topics I like and some I don't. Like politics. I don't like politics. I can't make it funny; it's too depressing with all these politicians.

So anyway, I go back and find the next. No good. All videos of other people being funny. I may enjoy this later, but it is not what I am looking for. Back to Google.

So this next site I don't like so much. Click. Click. Click. No topics. None. Zip. Just that phrase all over again.

Oh. There it is, Tiny tiny print. "view story"

Story? I wasn't looking for a story. Oh very well I click.

Yes this was it. These topics, they can be funny or not. Depends on how you see them. Like how to give your pet a pill. This is a topic.

Short topic if you ask me. There's the hide it in something, give it to the dog, he eats all but the pill.

End of the story. I need something meatier. We move on.

Prattle On - Teri Stricker

Ah drunk people. They are sad, but sometimes funny, it is true. Mostly I just wonder why we have to tell everyone we are drunk. This has been done though, a million times.

The thing is, it has to be something I see the funny in. And if I pick a topic that say, I heard Robin Williams do, I am apt to sound like HIM. Without all the jumping about, I am not so energetic as him.

So maybe I am stuck coming up with my own ideas. My own drivel. Darn. So much for the easy way out.

So, I log on to the ONLINE, I ask my friend Jon, the instigator, for a topic he says. "COON HUNTING."

HUH?

I've never been. I've never been hunting at all. I can't kill things. I can help butcher, I can package, but I can't pull the trigger. I am a softy. I can't help it. They are cute. They have a ready made mask.

A friend of mine had a pet raccoon. I don't advise this at all. They make huge messes for such little things. They can open cabinet doors. They pull everything out, onto the floor.

I had one jump out of a dumpster at me. I was emptying the garbage of course. He didn't like it landing on him. So he was scared, I was scared, he ran away, end of story.

So Jon, he is no help.

The redneck thing, Jeff Foxworthy does way better than me. I have found out I am a redneck because of him. I am not really surprised.

You've heard of this thing called "Buck Fever?" Aspirin doesn't help. My mother went deer hunting with my father once. She ejected all her shells onto the ground. None found the deer.

The deer probably looked at her knowingly. He'd seen it before.

However, I think I have found a topic now. Not hunting. My Dad could do hunting stories, not me, I could only tell his stories badly. But my mother, outdoors, it brings me to camping.

So we have to chapter. I know, I know, it is sad, ending a chapter. But we must, otherwise we go on and on and no one can go to the bathroom. Besides, my tea is empty. I keep trying to drink from an empty cup. This is not good. So let's chapter.

Prattle On - Teri Stricker
Chapter Thirty Five - Camping

So, camping. You might have gone camping. It is lots of fun when you are a kid. It is quite fun when you are a man, if my father is any indication. For a mother, not so much. For a woman who is scared of everything furry, even less.

My mother didn't like ANYTHING. I'm not just talking about snakes. Most women don't like snakes, I hear. Mom didn't like birds, bees, nothing. Anything could scare her.

The trip I am going to tell you about I was very young. It doesn't matter, I remember it. I remember it because it was a comedy of errors start to finish. I think it was also the last time we did any real camping. I was not surprised by this.

As a kid, you are going camping, you tell your friends. "We are camping this weekend!"

"Lucky!"

Yes yes yes! We will fish, we will jump in leaf piles we will, well we will do lots of fun things, of this I am sure.

We did not go to a campground. My father is a SERIOUS camper. No fellow camping children to play with. You drive out into the middle of nowhere and you camp. No merry line of campfires.

So first you find a spot. This is the middle of the woods. The ground is covered with leaves. My mother does not like this. She knows in those leaves are acorns, sticks, lumpy things.

She has brought a broom. I kid you not, she has a broom.

So she sweeps the area where the tent will be while Dad pulls the tent out of the trunk. In ten minutes there is flat dirt. Well mostly flat, anyway.

Now we stomp. "Come help, kids!"

Prattle On - Teri Stricker

We all stomp. This is fun. BROTHER and I stomp around, growling like bears, or at least like what we imagine bears sound like.

The tent takes an hour to set up. This is not because Dad doesn't know what he is doing, this is because BROTHER and I are helping. Without us, it would probably take ten minutes.

"Bring me the long pole."

"Daddy, there are six long poles! Which one?"

"It doesn't matter. They are all the same. Bring me one."

He is very patient with us, and there is laughter as I carry the pole wrong and run into two trees. Small trees, but big enough to stop my progress.

I am a six year old child, after all, not a rocket scientist.

My uncle and his family they are setting up somewhere out of sight. He and Dad will be spending a lot of time together. I don't remember the cousins being there, but they could have been, memory is funny like that.

There is a lake or a big pond, I don't know which, again out of sight.

The tent is up, then a nice fire. You can't camp without a fire. Tonight we'll roast marshmallows. I don't know if you can camp without marshmallows. I think that's illegal.

Dad brought his guitar, so at night there is music and singing. Mom is laughing a lot, this is good.

Bedtime is when you run out of things to talk about. So the family of four goes to the 10 x 8 tent, if it is that big. All I know for sure here is that it is small and cozy. Dad snores.

You hear crickets, frogs, something in the bushes. You can reach out and touch your parents, so this is not a problem. Nothing can hurt you with Daddy right there. At six Daddy is right up there with God.

So the next day we fish. Fishing at six is mostly asking Daddy to unsnag your line. You never knew this fishing thing was so hard. You are using a cane pole that is roughly three times as tall as you are. This is the small one.

For those of you not old like me, or not fishing folks, a cane pole is a long piece of bamboo. It is hollow and light. There is no reel. I suppose you could have a reel on it, but when you are six, this is just one more thing to break.

So in my case the line is tied to the end of the pole, and it is just long enough for me to manage to swing it out into the water, so I can watch my bopper.

This is camping and fun, so Daddy is not so serious with the fishing. Usually we go out on one of the bayous in a rowboat. I snag. Daddy tells me we will fix it when he's fished this spot out. So you play in the water a little, but no splashing, that will scare the fish.

After a while you get bored. You have caught one fish and snagged your line 300 times. You are hot and sweaty. So Daddy has BROTHER take you back to Mom.

We have to wait a bit. Mom is not at the tent. Oh dear here she comes.

"DAAAAAAAAD!"

Dad comes. Mother is running down the hill, her pants are at her ankles, and she is screeching. "SNAAAAAAAAAAAAAAKE!!!"

There are no bathrooms in the woods. I checked. There is an art to peeing in the woods if you are a girl. Things get in the way. But Mom has taught me. I do okay.

So now Dad has Mom calmed down, she has pulled up the pants, we are back sitting around where the fire was last night.

"Okay, what happened?"

So she had to go pee. She finds a tree to lean against, like she taught me. This helps take some of your weight off the legs. She took toilet paper with her. She will send Daddy to fetch that later.

She gets into the position, she pees. She finishes, but still there is this hiss. There should NOT be a hiss.

She looks down there is a snake. He is not really very happy about being pissed upon.

Now the adrenaline kicks in and she jumps up and runs. This is where we came in.

Daddy tried. He did. He tried very hard not to laugh. I watched him. I thought his face would explode before it burst out.

"It's NOT funny!"

But soon, the fear is all the way gone, and she is laughing too. This story will be told many times over the years.

So now the men folk have gone back to fishing, or perhaps they were after the giant turtle. At some point they caught it because we had turtle stew that weekend. BROTHER and I had the heart in a baggie all day Sunday I think it was. It is true. A turtle heart does keep beating long after it leaves the turtle.

In the meantime Mom and I are in the tent. She is doing crosswords or something, I don't remember. She was very good at crosswords. She quit school at sixteen to marry my father, but she did learn a lot while she was there.

My brother's bb gun is on the floor of the tent. I am six.

Another scream.

I have shot my mother in the ass with the bb gun. I am not her favorite person right this moment.

I don't know if I actually got her. I think if there was a bb embedded in her ass, we'd have wound up at the emergency room. But this is looking back. At the time, I was six, and I had just killed my mother.

I needed some comforting. So did she.

As you may have guessed, we somehow survived the camping trip, and went home on Sunday night.

We visited other people camping after that. We didn't go. I don't think I was surprised.

You have guessed it. Time to chapter, we are back home after all.

Chapter Thirty Six

I told you I grew up in Michigan, by a lake. What I didn't mention is we lived in an old house. It was the first house built on that road, it was probably a grass road then. Maybe a two track. Anyway it was old.

It was 3 bedrooms, which were not very big. You could fit the bed and the dressers. BROTHER got the smallest one. Looking back, I've had closets bigger than that room, since then.

So this house was built around 1900 or so. Wooden floors. Painted wooden floors because if they had ever been nice, they weren't now.

It had been updated before my parents bought it, so no lathe and plaster, it was drywall.

Originally it was built as a summer cottage. No one was supposed to live there in the winter. You can tell.

Originally it had a wrap around porch. By the time we moved in, the wraparound part had been closed in with windows, it's now part of the house. They didn't bring the floor up though, so you step down, or up. Or you trip.

It looked much like a sun room, I guess. All windows.

The bathroom and the laundry room were obviously afterthoughts. The laundry room had the pump, the washer and dryer, a work bench over the pump, and the hot water heater.

The bathroom was under the upstairs hall. The closet under the stairs was nearly as big as the bathroom. There was room in the bathroom for a "this is where we stack things" table, which was, in happier days, my mother's vanity table.

There was a sink bolted to the wall, the medicine cabinet above it, the toilet, the tub. No shower.

This house was heated by a Warm Morning stove. Natural gas. A space heater, in other words. No insulation, also no vents to the upstairs, but upstairs was quite warm anyway, heat rises.

Prattle On - Teri Stricker

The plumbing was in the crawlspace. The plumber had to be skinny and like to try and find leverage to loosen and tighten pipes on his back. This was Daddy.

There were holes behind the pump. There had to be, because this is how the chipmunks got in.

My dog Sandy did not like dog food. He ate table scraps. If it was human food, it was good. Mashed potatoes, of course meat, and even tomatoes, he didn't care. As long as it wasn't dog food.

I know. Don't feed your dog table scraps, they are bad for him. He was 17 years old when he died. Maybe if we hadn't fed him table scraps it would have been 20.

So the chipmunks would come in, and eat the dog food. We always had dog food. I don't know why, maybe for the chipmunks, the dog wouldn't eat it.

Sandy did NOT like the chipmunks eating it though. So we would be watching TV in the living room, Sandy is on the floor near someone's feet. Most times he didn't care whose, as long as there was someone going to trip when they tried to move.

Crunch crunch crunch. Sandy leaps to his feet. The wood floors have been covered in linoleum, so he slips and slides into the kitchen. The chipmunk waits for him. Then runs for the laundry room and the hole behind the pump.

Mom is standing on a chair. No, I don't know why. The chipmunk isn't heading this way, why would he?

Once though, she was in the dining room by the table. It was a kitchen table, fake wood plastic on metal legs. She jumped on the table. The legs gave out. This didn't hinder the chipmunk chase at all, but we did have to fix the table.

So Sandy slips and slides through the kitchen, after the chipmunk.

Then we go get him out from behind the pump where he has wedged himself.

Prattle On - Teri Stricker

Then there are the birds. There is no screen on the chimney. In the summer, obviously the heater wasn't running then.

So once in a while, a bird would come down the chimney, bang around in the stove until it found the opening in the back where there was supposed to be a metal plate, but there wasn't, and now it is flying around the house.

We are not talking vampire bats. We are talking a sparrow here. Little bird.

Mom barricades herself in the bathroom and we have to deal with the bird.

This isn't as hard as it sounds. They go for the windows. They want outside, after all and they can see it. They don't want to be in our house any more than Mom wants them there. So they get to the windows, and inevitably get tangled in the curtains.

We have Mom hand us a towel from the bathroom. We have to convince her the bird is nowhere near for this, but eventually we get the towel.

Now you go to the windows, and if he hasn't killed himself banging against the window over and over (most didn't), you get him in the towel and take it all outside.

You open the towel and run out of the way. The bird stands there and blinks a minute, gets his bearings and slows his heart, and flies away. Crisis over.

Except we have to go back to the bathroom and tell Mom she can come out now.

Then there's snakes. My brother was the one who took the garbage out. So it is just after garbage day, the can is empty, and my brother has caught a snake or two. So he put them in the garbage can until after school.

This is not a problem, right? Wrong.

Mom came home from work early. She cleans a bit. Takes out the garbage.

We come home, Mom is sitting on the sofa, the TV is going, she is doing crosswords.

"BROTHER go clean the back yard."

BROTHER is naturally mystified. "CLEAN the back yard?"

"Yes there is garbage, go pick it up."

I go to help. She is right. There is garbage. Everywhere, also the kitchen garbage can lying forlornly on it's side.

It's obvious she threw it straight up in the air. I am sympathetic. BROTHER is on his back on the grass laughing so hard I am thinking he is going to pull something.

My mother comes to the back door. "It is NOT funny."

Right.

Fast forward 20 years. I have moved into the house with MY family. I am getting ready for work. Kitty flies past me with something huge. I'm thinking a big bird.

It got away. I grab the cat, lock him in the bathroom, grab a towel while I am at it. I remember this drill.

A noise tells me it is in the laundry room. This is a BIG bird. It has a hooked beak. Oh dear. The towel doesn't seem like the best idea anymore. Okay. Well, before I can take care of the bird, I have to call work, tell them I will be late.

"Umtyfrat company"

"This is Teri. Can you tell BOSS I am going to be late? I've a young hawk in my house, I have to get it out before I can come in."

"A WHAT?"

"Hawk. You know hooked beak, carnivore. That. It can't be here when the kids get home after all, they could get hurt."

"This is one I've never heard of. How did it even get in?"

"I don't know, the cat won't tell me."

Anyway she obviously doesn't believe me. I realize this. So I grab the camera and take a picture of the hawk on my dryer, for evidence later.

Then I enter the room. My aim is to open the back door and herd him outside. He has other ideas.

He flies out into the kitchen, surprise surprise, ends up at that long row of windows.

Great.

So the towel becomes a herding device. Eventually I get him out the front door, he flies away. I go to work.

I have only one more animal story I can think of. This one was not in the house at least.

I'm 12 or so. We are in a rowboat on the bayou in front of my grandparents' house. Mom, me, Aunt, who is actually a cousin, and Cousin.

Anyone who is remotely a family member is Aunt or Uncle. Close friends are the same. Mr. or Mrs. Is too formal for daily wear and tear, but we must have respect. So the Aunt or Uncle.

Anyway, we are fishing. A baby duck, how cute. Little yellow fuzzy baby duck is running across the water to us. We see no other ducks.

It swims around the boat, runs into the boat, he wants IN the boat.

Cousin and I get into the water. It comes right to us. So we and the baby duck get into the boat. Mom is protecting her feet.

I told you everything made her nervous. This is no exception. I don't know what she thought this tiny thing was going to do to her feet.

We row around trying to find Mama duck. No dice. So now we have a duck. Aunt doesn't want a duck. Mom surely doesn't want a duck.

We go back to Grandma's, take care of the boat, go see Grandma. She too, has no need for a duck.

My father is living back in Michigan so we call. Yes, he will take the duck. We take it to him.

This duck was cute. It also thought it was a dog. It followed my Dad everywhere. The end of this story, it's as weird as the beginning.

He went hunting. WITH the duck. Most take a hunting dog. By now it is a grown up duck.

He left the gun and the duck in the tent, went to town for supplies.

He returned. Someone stole the gun AND the duck.

I can't make this stuff up. It happened. Really.

So time to chapter and find something else to tell you.

Prattle On - Teri Stricker
Chapter Thirty Seven – Sometimes I Was Smart

You are not supposed to have a favorite child. People do though. Otherwise, where on earth do you come up with "Daddy's Girl" or a "Mama's Boy"?

BROTHER was the favorite. I wasn't bitter. He was funny. Witty. Fun to be with. He was my favorite too. He was responsible. He helped Mom fix things. He babysat.

Except later, I learned that although I was supposed to be more like him, he was supposed to be like ME.

I was a straight A student. Honor roll. Rarely got in trouble. He was in the Principal's office often. They chatted. He was the class clown, I was teacher's pet.

So my mother would ask why I couldn't be more like my brother, and ask my brother why he couldn't be more like me.

I have no idea why we didn't hate each other.

I was good at school, and practically nothing else. He was good at practically everything else, not so good at the school.

He fixed things. Well, he meant to. One slice didn't work in the toaster. When he got done there were extra parts. Now nothing worked. Oh well.

Now my brother has moved out and he is an adult. It's just me and Mom.

My mother was not into technology. Anything with wires worried her. Back during this time we are dabbling in, there was no cable TV. We had an antenna.

My mother didn't know how it worked. She didn't have to. She turned on the TV, it worked.

One day after moving the TV to sweep under it, it did NOT work.

She played with the vertical, the horizontal, she slapped it. No change.

I am 14. I fear nothing. "Mom, I know what's wrong. The antenna wire is disconnected."

"Get away from there you'll electrocute yourself."

I shake my head. "Mom, there's not a danger of that with an antenna wire."

"Go upstairs, I am trying to think."

Ok. I go upstairs. I write my poems of angst, or maybe I read. It was long ago, I don't remember for sure.

An hour passes. "Teri come here."

I come. That's what you do when your mother calls if you don't want to get in trouble.

She has unplugged the TV at some point. She has the antenna wire in her hand. She is touching it to everywhere on the TV but where it goes. I think if there is a way to electrocute yourself with an antenna wire on an unplugged TV, she would find it.

"Where does this damn thing go?"

I come around, I look.

"See these screws?"

"Those don't look like they GO to anything."

"Well they do. See these two, it says VHF, and these two, it says UHF. The wires there on the UHF, that's going to the rabbit ears up top. That's PBS."

She looks at me with a new form of respect.

"How do you know this?"

"I don't know I just picked it up somewhere I guess."

I have inherited BROTHER's radio. It is brown. It plugs into the wall, but it can also take a 9 volt battery. Well, it could once. There are two bare wires where the battery wire once was now. The cover to this area has been missing for years.

You turn it on nothing happens. You hit it, it comes on. This works until you want to turn it off, then the same thing applies.

After about a year I am sick of knocking the radio onto the floor to turn it on and off. So I go into the back of it.

There are wires, and doodads and things. In this case, there is a loose wire. I tighten it. No more hitting the radio. It works. I am a genius, I think. Of course I did, I was a teenager. You are a teenager, you know everything.

I don't miss those days, knowing everything is a big responsibility.

Now we must chapter. I am out of technology from childhood.

Prattle On - Teri Stricker
Chapter Thirty Eight – School Shopping and Dances

In high school there are dances. I didn't go to many. No date. But for some reason, GIGI and I went to the homecoming dance in tenth grade. Stag. Guys go stag, girls don't. Or not then anyway. We did.

We actually had more fun than with a date. I know I watched. Now of course GIGI and I didn't dance the slow dances. Neither of us were wearing dresses as nice as the other girls. I was wearing this god awful brown thing my mother had found. No really this was UGLY. But it was a dress.

I didn't like dresses. Tomboy, remember? So this was what I had. Anyway I watched the other kids too, I was a people watcher even then. Plus, I was a bit jealous. At first.

First they sit at tables and look at each other nervously. Not sure what to say to each other, this is a date and all. For some it is a FIRST date.

Some of the girls are in high heels for the first time other than wearing their mom's when mom isn't looking.

Soon, they figure out it's safer in a group, so now they go to several couples to a table. Now there is conversation. This looks more fun.

We've been here an hour, GIGI and I are the only ones who have danced. The guys don't know how to ask their dates, or something.

I don't know, this is what I guess.

Somewhere into the second hour, they have loosened up. The group thing. So slowly they wander out onto the floor.

By the end of the dance they are all having fun too. But GIGI and I had fun FIRST. We leave early, we are walking, and we have danced enough. We've been to a dance stag, and we have lived. We are full of ourselves.

Getting school clothes was almost the only time I shopped with my mother, other than for groceries.

Grocery shopping consisted of chasing my mother down the aisles. That woman could MOVE. She wasted no time, she had the list, she had the clicker to be sure of how much she was spending.

She didn't browse. You browse you might buy something that isn't on the list. So we race through the store.

Shopping for clothes is different, this takes time.

I hated it. I hated the clothes. I hated it all. She had a love affair with polyester pants with gathered elastic waists. I did not. I wanted jeans.

"Everyone wears jeans, Mom."

"I don't wear jeans, you don't wear jeans, EVERYONE does not wear jeans. You are not going to look like a farm worker."

Now I am mystified. What on earth is a farm worker? And what is wrong with them? I am smart enough not to ask. Tomorrow I'll go to the library and look it up. Which won't help, the words tell you all you are going to get. Farm Worker – someone who works on a farm. It doesn't tell you what is wrong with them, or why you shouldn't dress like them.

So I have the polyester pants with the beaded seam down the leg. No wonder I was an outcast.

By the time I was a teen, we had graduated to dress pants at least. No beaded seam. This is still not cool, it is not jeans. But I've done this shopping thing before, I know better than to whine. It wastes more time, and accomplishes nothing.

Now I am not a little girl so we have to get bras. My mother pulls measuring tape out of her purse. "We need to measure."

"In the middle of the AISLE? No. I am definitely not doing this."

"What? You think other women don't get bras?"

"I don't think they measure themselves in the store aisle. In fact, I'm sure of it."

"Fine, we'll go to the fitting room."

Lord. So we find out my size and all, and we return to the dainties aisle.

Mother grabs a package of bras. Hearts and flowers.

"MOM!"

"Now what?"

"That is gross."

"Bras are not gross. It's part of being a woman. You wear a bra you don't black an eye running."

I look down. I am quite sure I'm in no danger of a black eye.

"It's not the wearing of a bra, I get that. Does it have to be so, so GIRLY?"

"For pity's sake Teri you want it to be BOY EEE? We've had this talk, I'm pretty sure you know boys don't wear bras."

Lord. Did this woman forget EVERYTHING about being young? She can't be THAT old, can she?

You take a deep breath. "How about this over here, it's plain, it's simple, no flowers."

"That is expensive. You think I am made of money? Who is going to see anyway? It goes under your clothing."

I could mention the locker room, but I know this mood. Time to shut up and give in.

So you have the hearts and flowers bras. In the cart, where ANYONE can see. While Mom is moving on to the panties, you quickly throw the pants over them. There. That's better.

The underwear is less traumatic. We had the briefs versus bikini argument last year. She has agreed I don't need to wear underwear that go up to my neck. Thank goodness. She has actually listened to how I don't like the hearts and the flowers, she just can't afford to buy the other ones. I learn this maybe ten years after the fact.

So this is easier. She picks a package of bikini underwear, colored, no lace, no hearts, no flowers.

"Thanks Mom."

Next we go to the supplies. This was no big deal when I was a kid. A notebook. Some pencils. However, this year Mom splurges and buys me a tote bag for my books.

I live exactly a mile from the school. This means a bus comes. However, It is close enough to walk. I usually ride in the morning, and walk home in the afternoon.

I walk home in the afternoon because on the way home is the library.

My mother knows this. She often beats me home because I can spend hours in a library. I come home with a stack of books. She has been joking if I had one more book I'd have to grow longer arms.

Mom likes that I read, and also she does NOT like that I read. I get INTO a book. I'm there, in whatever world is being painted. She talks to me, there is nothing. She grabs the book out of my hand, voila she has my attention.

She's also lost my place, but this is not the time to complain about it. Not if you don't want a fat lip or something.

Another thing about teenagers, they space out. I did it. Empty the ashtray in the sink, throw the fork in the garbage. My kids did it. It's a phase. It passes. Well, for some of us. Some I think, maybe not.

I think we have a chapter. How about that. Let's do it.

Prattle On - Teri Stricker
Chapter Thirty Nine - Drinking

I don't drink much. I think I said. I had my one falling down drunk thing, sometimes I get tipsy, that's as good as it gets.

So my kids never saw me drunk. Never. It didn't happen. The few times I got tipsy, I got home after they went to bed. So the babysitter saw me tipsy, not my kids.

No hangovers, nothing. Sometimes DAD and I might have a glass of wine at dinner. That was about it.

Now we come to my 40 h'birthday. DAD has a gig, he is in a band.

I am being "a good sport." I have an abscessed tooth. Nothing helps that. You drink water, a lot of water. You feel like a whale you are so bloated. But I am going to the gig. I'll take some pictures, do some video, even though he will hate both.

I don't have steady hands. My videos will make you nauseous, they jerk about. My pictures are rarely wonderfully clear. I also take pictures of all the wrong things, never what DAD wanted me to take pictures of.

So I am there at the table with the lead singer's wife. She needs a name. Let's call her Emma. Her name is not Emma, doesn't even rhyme with Emma. She will probably read this and ask me why I couldn't pick a prettier name. I don't know, I'm not so good with pretty.

Emma is pretty. She is blonde, nice shape, the guys like to look at her. She has eyes only for her husband though, this is how it should be. Emma is nice, and she is funny. We sing along at the table, we make jokes.

Our job as the head groupies is we greet the other band followers, and we are the first ones to get out on the dance floor. This is because no one wants to be the first. They might look stupid, they think, and it is too early in the evening for them to be drunk and not care.

Prattle On - Teri Stricker

I order a drink. During the first set Lead Singer guy announces it is my birthday. Half the people in the bar sent me a drink.

So since I now have free drinks I am going to drink until my abscess doesn't hurt.

Mind you, I am not drunk. At the end of the night I still can help my husband with the tearing down and the toting of equipment. If I was drunk, he wouldn't let me anywhere near it. I told you, he's smart.

So we get home. My son, he stays up late all the time. It's the weekend, and he is watching some crap on cable. We sit down in the living room and talk.

I was tipsy. He was amazed. He claims I am drunk. I am probably impaired enough that I shouldn't drive, were that an issue, but I'm not reeling around bouncing off walls. There may be a slight slur to my speech I don't know.

So he has to giggle and carry on. And wake up half the family to show them his drunken mother.

Sheesh.

It's probably one of his funniest memories, I don't know. All I know is he got a huge kick out of it.

Then I look at my childhood. Drunk was normal. My mother was drunk often. My father, he never SEEMED drunk, but he drank a lot.

I was good at pouring beer into a glass without too much foam. Mom had to have a glass. Drinking out of the can was less classy or something, I don't know. Maybe there was no reason, other than, she likes a glass.

Family gatherings, there was a lot of drunk going on as well. By the time my kids grew up and we went to these things, all of the drinkers had gone on the wagon or died.

So they weren't exposed to this. I look at the contrast between my childhood and theirs just on this one thing and it is vast.

I manage to have fun sober, that's all. I'm a happy person, so I'm not trying to escape from emotional pain. I am relatively healthy, so I don't have to escape physical pain. Unlike my mother, I'm not bipolar so there is also no self-medication reason.

I didn't want to become an alcoholic, but neither does any child of an alcoholic. Many still do it. There was no conscious thing on my part. I just always stop when I feel that buzz. The buzz is enough. No need to get to where I can't walk or talk.

The other thing is I don't like beer. I don't like most of the wines. So when I drink it's the liqueurs. Baileys, Kahlua and crème these are expensive.

Also you get in more trouble now. As you should. My mother, she parked her car on top of a snow bank. I remember this conversation.

"Just HOW did you do this?"

"I don't know. I don't remember a snow bank."

"Well, the snow will melt, we'll get it."

There was also a tree that jumped out into the road. Except when it was over, she was in someone's front yard, and so was the tree.

These were funny stories later, only because no one got hurt, including Mom.

Times were different then, drinking was a bigger part of life. My parents socialized much more than I do, spent more time in bars, playing pool, socializing.

So, I don't drink much. I was also always very careful what I said to my children. I grew up and found some self-confidence and all, that didn't mean that I had to give my children those same hurdles to jump. I probably gave them some new ones. They haven't mentioned it.

Time to chapter, you are right.

Prattle On – Teri Stricker
Chapter Forty – Be Nice, It Can't Hurt

Morning again. Wow. That's like every day. So is night. Amazing. Every 24 hours you hit the same exact time. I know, because my alarm goes off.

DAD doesn't set the alarm, and he doesn't turn it off. He pats me instead. "You going to turn that off?"

Actually, I made that up. That doesn't happen. That doesn't happen because he sleeps through it. If he happens to be on his back his snore is actually louder than the alarm.

Then there is SLSIL's alarm. He works all different hours. So he forgets it is set on days off. When an alarm in the house goes off, first it seeps into your brain, you don't know what you are hearing.

Eventually you say "what is that noise?"

So you track it down. You have to then futz with this unfamiliar alarm clock to turn it off. You mutter a bit. This happens about once a week.

Today is Veteran's Day. I am a veteran. Online in the chat rooms people thank us for serving. That's nice.

They are thinking mostly of those who got shot at and survived though. I am not one of those.

Life is this thing, you know? It's not always nice. There is war, and hunger, and general not happy things going on.

But these things, they have always been. You can't spend all of your time thinking about them, you will get depressed a lot.

You give to the Salvation Army, you maybe send care packages to the troops, this is nice.

Mostly we just live, don't we? We work, we dance, we talk to people. There's nothing wrong with that. I am not responsible for the war and the hunger, neither are you.

DAD and I have helped people here and there, in ways that we can. A car is in a ditch, you stop, offer to help. Sometimes all they need is for you to call a tow truck or something. But they appreciate that you cared enough to stop.

You see someone carrying too much, you offer to help carry a little of it. Someone drops something, you pick it up and hand it to them. These are small things. But they are NICE small things.

There is nothing wrong with being nice, is there?

THEY say "nice guys finish last." Maybe so. I would still rather be nice.

When we moved back to where I grew up, I knew my neighbors. These days, you really don't. You are all busy. And we move more often. Few kids today grow up in one house over 20 years.

Anyway they had a daughter who had a baby. It was a difficult birth, and the child had problems. Luckily there was medicine and these things.

This is when I started to get close to them. They all worked. At the time I was not working. I was raising the kids and helping DAD with his business. He was out of town a lot during this time.

I took over the baby gift, I see the situation.

The new mother can't move very well, although many things she can do for her baby without getting up if the materials are nearby.

So I say what can I do? Well, I can go over there and visit when everyone else is at work. I can fetch things. This isn't so hard. It's only next door, so my kids can find me. This is good.

Over the years we lived there, this was a two way street. They helped me as well. If I needed a ride, one of them was happy to do so. We didn't have a scoreboard or anything. "You did this, so I'll do that." Friendship doesn't work that way. Not the good ones anyway.

Prattle On - Teri Stricker

They jokingly called me Mr. Wilson. This was a character on a sitcom who was very smart. I helped with their computer, I helped with the stereo.

When my water pump bit the dust, they helped me by letting me hook up to their faucet and get water. I babysat occasionally, this little baby as she grew.

She was a cutie. Most little kids are.

So being nice, you don't always wind up last. A good friendship came of this. They were nice too! Imagine that.

Also when I was working, this household next door, they all worked different times. So someone was usually at home. So my children had someone to go to if there was a problem, and they kept an eye out even when there wasn't.

So, my kids would get in trouble when I got home. "How did you know I did that."

"I'm a mother, I know."

I was at work when my son got hurt with the golf club. The neighbor saw to him until DAD could get home. She was a nurse, she knew the questions to ask.

The daughter, the one with the difficult birth, she knew too.

My son said later he was asked the same questions 4 times. So I knew when I spoke to them on the phone and they said no signs of concussion or anything, they knew what they were talking about.

We still had to take him to the doctor, and I went home for this, but at least it wasn't a mad rush, I knew he was in good hands.

I miss them.

The neighbors here I don't know. I've lived here a year and a half; they have changed already to new neighbors.

Our friends now are usually co-workers or something. And there are the ONLINE friends. So you can chat. You have your coffee, you chat. It's not so bad.

Of course it isn't the same. You don't ever know if you KNOW these people. They don't know if they know YOU. You might know their first name. You talk. But you have someone to rant to about how the GIRL never ever puts away the peanut butter, you know?

You realize it is time to chapter. Yes. Me too.

Chapter Forty One – ONLINE Life

So there is the Online. I talk there much like I am talking to you. Except it is not so one sided of course. They get to say something too.

People online, they are the same as people offline, except you can't judge them by what they are wearing, or if they meet your eyes when they talk. It is text.

Even in voice, EVEN If you have the cams on and you are talking, they can't very well look you in the eye even if they want to.

So I chat, I sing. My online friends have heard a lot of what I've told you. It's just not all been in one place.

In Second Life, this 3D world, I mentioned, you still chat, talk, converse. You have an avatar. I call it a Barbie doll, it looks like one.

The avatars are as varied as the people. Some who have seen me say it looks a bit like me, my Barbie. But it is still not me. I am sitting at the keyboard in my sweats. The avatar looks chic. Why not? Her clothes are cheap.

People throw parties, there is music and chat. There are gestures. This means I can type like "/app" and there is applause at the end of a friend's song. It is nice.

Some funny things happen, like since when I sing here, Barbie can fall off the stage. Then while I am singing and figuring out what will be the next song, I also have to get her back on the stage. Little things.

I was once invited to a party for Halloween. "Can you come to my party?"

"I don't know. When is this party.?" It is presently 7AM.

She says "8:30"

I assume PM. Parties are usually afternoon, or night. So sure.

She didn't. She meant AM. I am thinking she decided this at the last minute. So at 8:30AM she sends me the Teleport. In SL you walk your Barbie, you fly your Barbie, or you teleport. 5 people show up. We are in costume. Well, our BARBIES are in costume, I am still in my sweats at the keyboard.

She is complaining no one is here. This makes those of us who are here, very special, you understand.

So we stand. We stare at each other. The minutes tick by.

Then she says. "We need music, Teri you want to sing?"

OK. This is not the best planned party I am thinking. I am trying to imagine how this would work in real life. Of course, you couldn't teleport to a party in Real life you'd have to drive.

In Real life also, you don't have your equipment handy in such a situation either. Believe it or not, I don't run about with my microphone and mixer, etc. in my back pocket. Or even in my purse.

I am a woman, there is PLENTY in my purse, just not these things. Also not the kitchen sink.

My cable went down. I was saved. But it was interesting, I have to admit.

You meet a wide selection of people. You have both girls and guys hitting on you, occasionally. I'm not offended either way, I still say no. I am still married, no matter who asks, and this online sex, this cyber sex, I don't get. I never have. I doubt I ever will.

In Second Life, this is like Barbie and Ken having sex. Ew.

Second Life has everything. There are role playing simulators where you pretend you are knights or damsels or whatever.

There are stores, there are clubs with music. There are MOVIE theaters.

Prattle On - Teri Stricker

I don't understand this one so much. I can watch a movie full size on my computer screen. I don't need this mini version. Also, there is no popcorn. The popcorn and the big screen are why people go to the movies. So, I don't get it. Except it was probably fun to create. That part I get.

In real life there are all sorts of people too, I am just not exposed to most of them. Like these Goth folks. I don't see many in RL, they are all over SL.

There are these people who have this domination thing. One guy he talks about his girl and calls her his pet. She calls him "Master."

So much for the feminist movement, I am thinking. My husband couldn't even get me to have the word "obey" in the wedding vows; I am definitely NOT calling him "Master". I am an independent person. In a marriage you depend on each other, but this is different. But to become someone's pet, this is not going to happen for me.

The live in their own spots and all, but online the people mix more.

There are exotic dancers, there are strippers. This I don't get either. You are in Second Life. You can wear any avatar you want. You want to see a naked woman, go home, put on a naked woman. Look. Why you need to see this one? I don't know.

Barbie and Ken, they have no parts. No BITS some call them. These parts you can buy. Anyone can. You don't have to be a man to buy a certain attachment.

So a male avatar comes up waving his attachment, this doesn't impress me. I can get one. I don't want one, but I can get one. I don't need his.

So even though I wander this virtual world, and I sing in it, my feet are firmly planted in the real life.

Some people they live in Second Life like they wish they could live in the real one. They live in mansions, or castles. They wear fancy clothing, all of that.

I see nothing wrong with it. As long as they know the difference. Sometimes you wonder if they do.

Prattle On - Teri Stricker

So you meet a variety of people you wouldn't meet in the real world. It is safer this way. You don't have to go to the bad part of town, or drive 50 miles to meet them. Some are very nice, yes, even the domination people. I just don't want to be one of them.

Online you are who you want to be. You can be fat in real life, but unless you tell people, they don't know. Also your disabilities if you have them, don't count here. After all, you don't need your legs here. You have Barbie, and her legs work.

I am not disabled. I still enjoy. I am me wherever I go, I don't know how to be anyone else. Well, when I am on stage, I am just a louder me I guess, a more outgoing me.

But not everyone is who they say they are. Some want you to believe they are famous people, just in the online on the sly. Maybe they are. Maybe they aren't. If I like this person I don't care whether they are famous or not anyway. We are just talking after all.

Famous people, they are just people, after all. We just know who they are.

Most just are who they wish they were online. Typing is easier for some than talking. You can think about what you want to say, and how you want to say it. This sort of thing. I am sure some are funnier online.

If you are the class misfit, you don't have to tell people online. You can tell them you are the head cheerleader.

This can be dangerous as well. I've met a person or two that I knew online, and nothing bad happened, don't get me wrong. But read the news, sometimes these folks aren't so nice.

So you have to be careful. Even people you meet in real life, what do you know about them at the beginning? Nothing. So be careful. Don't go meeting them in private places.

Many groups have get togethers. These are usually pretty safe, there are a lot of you in one place, meeting each other.

You feel like you know these people, some you've chatted with for years. But you have to remember you DON'T know these people. Not really.

There are happy tales. Some people met the people they wound up marrying online. But there is also the ones who met their online love and lost all their money, trusting too much.

You can have the same problems falling for someone in the bar. Just be careful, this is all I am saying.

Yes it is probably time to chapter again. I noticed this. Let's do it.

Chapter Forty Two – Parenthood (I survived)

Kids get bored. REALLY bored. They have to tell you about it.

"I'm bored."

You've bought them enough toys to fill the Titanic, but they are bored. You tell them so. They go into their room for about 5 minutes.

"I am bored to DEATH!"

"Really? You are the healthiest corpse I've ever seen."

Sigh.

This is not just any sigh. This involves the entire body. The eyes glaze over first. Then the pout. The chest and shoulders heave up and down into this tremendous sigh.

They are obviously about to die.

"Do one of those 5000 puzzles I bought you."

"Mom those are boring."

Forget they begged you for each of them, they've done two.

"Go outside, catch something. Maybe you'll luck out, get bit by a rabid duck, and we can go to the hospital."

Now they laugh, a little. They walk away muttering about how I just don't understand.

I probably don't.

They manage to stretch it out to 8 minutes this time. "Mom I'm so bored!"

"So Play Monopoly with your brother."

BOY pipes up from his station in front of the television. "*I* am not bored."

Great.

"But you love Monopoly." I say coaxingly.

"I love spaghetti too, but I'm not in the mood for THAT right now either."

Where did I get this child? Oh yeah, he got this smart aleck thing from me. Except I rarely dared to actually SAY them.

Now GIRL sits on the arm of the sofa. "Bored. Bored. Really bored. Fantastically bored Tremendous-"

BOY looks at her. "You don't shut up you are going to be dead."

The sigh again. "Well at least I won't be BORED then."

Once, I was at a loss as to how to amuse this child. Then I learned the value of chores.

"Well, the kitchen floor could use a good mopping. Go do that."

"That's not FUN."

"No, but you won't be here irritating us all with how bored you are. Hop to it."

Not only does the floor get mopped, but afterwards she escapes and finds something to do.

It works. You note this for the next bored extravaganza.

Now I heard all the jokes about teenage girls always on the phone. GIRL did not get her own phone line. However things have changed a bit. Back when I was a teenage girl there was call a friend and chat.

Now one friend is not enough, she has to CONFERENCE call. Except no one told the parents about this.

So I am looking at the phone bill. "Hon, what are all these 3 way calling charges?"

DAD sits up. "Let me see." As if seeing the piece of paper will explain.

He is racking his brain for some business call he might have made.

Girl whooshes into the room. Really. You feel the air current, I tell you.

"I don't know. I don't think I've had to make a 3 way call in months."

GIRL plops on the sofa next to DAD. "How can you LIVE without 3 way?"

I spin my chair away from the desk and look at her. "So this $50 in 3 way belongs to you, young lady?"

Now she is not so whooshy. "Wow. That costs money?"

"Everything on God's green earth costs money. You will stop with the 3 way."

"But MOM! We HAVE to be able to talk all together. I mean we HAVE to."

"Then let one of them initiate it. Let THEIR parents pay for it. WE are not made of money."

Here is the sigh again.

The 3 ways came to a grinding halt, because it seems, THEIR parents were also not made of money.

When I was a kid, calling your parent at work was for emergencies. They could get fired for too many personal calls.

When my kids were young, first we had a pager. Well, DAD had a pager. So he would go to the store, and get a page. He would call from the pay phone to hear;

"Dad, can I have a piece of cake?"

He answered the question, finished whatever he was doing. He was too nice.

Now we graduate to cell phones. The kids are teenagers. I am working as a PC tech, I am at a user's desk while they are explaining this error they got and didn't write down, or leave up for me.

My cell phone rings.

I answer.

"Mom, can I have that last piece of cake?"

"GIRL, do you know where I am?"

"What does this have to do with cake?"

"I am at work." The user is grinning knowingly at her desk. I'm thinking she too, has had this conversation.

"When I am at work, this means you call me with important questions, like where is the first aide kit?"

"This IS important!"

"No, the world will not end if that cake is not eaten. You will not die a tragic death. There will be no blood. But there will be blood flowing if you do not get off the phone right this instant."

Click.

The great thing about these wireless phones... there is no more slamming the phone down.

I never got that anyway. You slam it as hard as you want; the person you hung up on still hears a quiet click.

So we shall chapter and talk about phones. I know, you are dying to hear about phones.

Prattle On - Teri Stricker
Chapter Forty Three – Phones Past and Present

When I was young, phones were connected to the wall. You had so many feet to pace with it, and that was it. Ours was in the kitchen.

There is no comfortable way to have a long conversation. Mom wouldn't buy I 50 foot chord so that I could sit on the sofa. Kitchen chairs are HARD, and kitchen chairy. So, I didn't spend hours on the phone.

The phone rang. BRRRRRING. That's it. No song, no choosing out of 17 styles of ringers, just BRRRRNG. It was loud and jarring, just like it was supposed to be.

Some people had more than one phone, but they were all plugged into the wall. No one I knew had an answering machine either.

There was no such thing as call waiting. You called while someone was on the phone, you got a busy signal. This sounds like a dial tone stuttering, basically.

If you left the phone off the hook, or the cat batted it off the cradle, you would soon hear "WAH WAH WAH WAH". This too is loud and jarring. Otherwise you wouldn't hear it from two rooms away.

This wasn't so bad. There was no such thing as a cell phone. People could not call you if you were in your car. They just had to wait until you got back home. There was no caller ID either. You didn't know anyone called. If they called and got the ring ring ring, and they felt it was important, they would call back later, that's all.

The world didn't end when they didn't reach you.

Somewhere in my teenage years there were car phones for those busy executives. These were much bigger than a credit card. They were heavy. You left them in the car, you didn't haul them into the store, or gas station, or whatever.

As a teenager they also came out with remote controls. WE didn't have one. I was the remote control. "Teri, turn the channel."

Prattle On - Teri Stricker

When I graduated from high school and went into the Navy, by now we had push button phones. They were still connected to the wall though. You couldn't wander down the street chatting with anyone.

Now, we have an area code, an exchange, and the number. That's what they call these 10 numbers we are assigned.

In the Azores, they had 4 numbers. That was it. Four digits to dial to talk to anyone on the base. Maybe even on the whole island, I don't know. I didn't call anyone else. In fact, I didn't call anyone at all.

If I did have to call someone we had a phone in a phone booth in the barracks. You didn't have to pay it, the booth was just to give you privacy.

My room mate decided we needed a phone. I said, no, it sounds like YOU need a phone, because I haven't felt a huge need for one.

So she got a phone. Now she can call her boyfriend and lay on the bed and talk, or whatever. No problem.

These phones, you can't unplug them from the wall. No simple little jack to unplug it. The same is true for the handset. You can't disconnect it from the phone.

Fast forward to two days after we got the phone. It is 1AM and both of us have to work in the morning.

It rings.

"Hello?"

"I need to talk to Juan."

"There is no Juan here, I'm afraid you have the wrong number."

"I know he is there! You tell him to call me or there is going to be trouble!"

This is all in a Portuguese accent, well HER end anyway.

"Senora, I beg to disagree. There is no Juan here."

"Senorita, I know you have been trying to steal my husband. It won't work. Always he plays outside, but he knows when it is time to come inside. You give him my message."

Finally you say "no Juan here" and hang up

She calls back.

You have much the same conversation. You hang up.

She calls back. She is getting angrier, and so are you, since you don't know this Juan.

So now you take the phone off the hook.

WAH WAH WAH.

So now you try to bury it in a drawer under the clothes.

It doesn't even seem to muffle it much.

You look at your room mate who is no happier than you are, and you decide not to tell her this is all her fault.

How was she to know she would get the old number of this Juan's girlfriend?

You got to the point of picking it up and hanging it up, but this still doesn't allow you to sleep.

Finally, it is 2AM. I take the phone.

"Look lady it's 2AM there is no Juan here. Let a poor girl sleep already."

"I KNOW he is there."

"Good, then you come fetch him. He's shitfaced. Just no more calls."

I hang up.

You STILL don't get to sleep until 3 AM because you are expecting that phone to ring again. It does not. Perhaps she found her Juan.

Today we have cell phones. People can reach you anywhere. Well, not anywhere. I refuse to take the phone to the bathroom. People can just wait.

We have voicemail, caller id, we have everything. We have wireless phones, so although the base is connected to the wall, the handset is free, we can carry it anywhere in the house, even out into the yard a little.

It is convenient, yes. The only problem is NOW you are always available. Going out of the house no longer means leaving the cares of the telephone behind it comes with.

This is good when DAD goes to the store and I remember something not on his list. It is bad when you are at Walmart with DAD, or anywhere you've escaped from the family to.

The phone rings. It is GIRL.

You answer.

"Where are you?"

"I am at Walmart."

"What are you doing?"

What am I DOING? GIRL has never gotten over this bored thing, and this question is a clue that this is her present problem.

"We have decided we are moving into Walmart. It is less crowded than the house."

"Oh Mom!" that disgusted tone she uses when I am pulling her leg in such an obvious way.

"Well, you asked a question you know the answer to. I have to tease. What do you need?"

"I'm bored. When are you coming home?"

"Go see what your children are into. This will keep the boredom away. Read them a story. As to when we'll be home, that depends on how long I am standing here not shopping, talking to you."

"Okay, okay. Shop. Can you get me some chocolate?"

"Will it end this conversation?"

"Yes."

"Then I can get you some chocolate."

DAD is smiling. I am a softie. He knows this.

"We should hurry and get what we need and get out of here, then." He says.

"No, we shouldn't. We should browse. We should take our time. GIRL is over 21 and has two children. She shouldn't need us right there constantly." I say.

"Fine. You are right. As usual."

So we rush through the shopping and go home.

We find GIRL and the children happily watching the sponge guy. Bob. He has square pants. We needn't have rushed. We weren't GOING to rush. We decided not to, remember? We did it anyway. Do you ever stop being a parent? I'm thinking no.

In the meantime, we have to chapter again, don't we?

Chapter Forty Four – Repeat After Me, Children Are Precious

Children are precious. They are a treasure. They are also a pain in the neck.

If you have an only child, they are bored. If you have more than one, they are also bored. The difference is, when they are bored SIBLINGS, they fight. The fights aren't boring. To them.

"MOM!"

"Yes my precious child, what is it?"

"BOY won't give me the remote!"

I look to BOY. "Why will you not give GIRL the remote?"

"I am WATCHING this."

"I see." It is some cartoon. Bugs Bunny in a diaper.

"And GIRL, what do you want to watch?"

It is all very serious to her. "ANYTHING but this!"

"Good. It is settled. GIRL, go watch the grass grow. It is not this."

Now, she does not go watch the grass grow, but she does know that pushing this issue is not the smartest course. So she wanders to her room and grumbles about how unfair I am.

This means I am being a good mother. If your kids like you, you are not parenting. At least, that's what my mother always said.

Children get in front of the television, they are gone. Totally. They have crawled inside there somewhere.

DAD comes into the room. "BOY, those dishes need doing."

Crickets.

"BOY!"

More crickets.

Prattle On - Teri Stricker

Eventually after five minutes of this, he taps him on the arm. He comes back. "Hi DAD! When did you get home?"

I don't do this. I haven't done this since they were five. I enter the room; pick up the remote, turn off the TV.

They turn around, their eyes full of who they are. Simple. Now we can have a conversation.

"What did you turn that off for?"

"I wanted to talk to you."

"You don't do that to DAD!"

"No, because he doesn't go into the Twilight Zone when the television is on."

They know the Twilight Zone from other conversations. Most of these are exactly like this one.

"Okay." BOY says. "What do you want?"

"World Peace. However, right this instant, I will be satisfied with the garbage going out."

This works. I don't frustrate myself talking to walls, and they go to do what you ask them to do in the interest of getting the television back on.

BOY is very smart. Like DAD. This seems to mean talking to the school often. There is always something. When your child is smarter than his teacher, this creates conflict.

Also, the teacher has no control in the classroom.

BOY lies on occasion, like any kid, but overall he is very honest. He has a keen sense of fair play as well, and he will stick up for what he thinks is right. I'd like to take credit for this, but I can't. It is built in. At two he was the same way. He will not get another kid into trouble for what he has done. He will HIDE something, but once it is out, he owns up.

So there is a call from the principal. DAD is on a first name basis since we moved to this school district.

"BOY was in a fight today, so I have to suspend him."

"Oh? What was the fight about?"

"This doesn't matter."

"No? I beg to differ." Says DAD. "But I will come down, obviously BOY is there in your office."

So we go.

DAD sits down, says hello to the principal, then turns to BOY. "So what happened this time?"

It seems these kids, in the classroom, daily are knocking his books out of his hands as he goes to his desk. And other things, always within sight of a staff member. He has complained.

The principal starts to speak, DAD holds up a hand. Wait. "And you told one of these teachers of your problem just in case they were all struck blind by your beauty?"

"I told Mr. L. He said 'Boys will be boys'."

Now DAD turns to the Principal. "You are suspending him for this, I think not. If the problem had been handled before the frustration level peaked, there would have been no fight.

"Now, DAD, we can't blame faculty for .."

"For not knowing what is going on in their own classrooms? Yes, we can."

I am silent. My input isn't needed after all; DAD has become a pro at this.

BOY is not suspended. However, I don't think these teachers were ever told to pay attention either.

I don't understand this. I've seen it time and time again, and I don't understand. I got picked on out on the playground, this I understand. NEVER in the classroom. You so much as whispered to a friend in the classroom the teacher put a stop to it.

Now, they throw things through the air, hit someone in the back of the head, whatever, the teacher doesn't notice. Why not? I mean, they are there to teach, not to day care, but this is obvious stuff. How is someone learning if they are slapping each other around?

Prattle On - Teri Stricker

My teachers turned their backs to write on the board. This gave us maybe 30 seconds to act up. They kept turning to look at us. They don't do this anymore? What?

BOY was almost suspended a number of times, and ACTUALLY suspended once. He owned up. He was having a bad day, and he did the wrong thing. He blamed no one for this. I told you, he has this sense of fair play. This is also why when other things happen, we believe him.

GIRL on the other hand, is another kind of treasure. She lies. A normal kid, in other words. When she was little you could catch her red handed, she would still lie.

You catch them with cookies. She is 5, he is three.

"Why did you steal cookies?"

BOY; "We wanted cookies. We knew you'd say no."

GIRL; "We DIDN'T"

"What is this in your hand, a vacuum? It looks like a cookie."

She was never a good liar, however, which made my job easier. She CLAIMS I caught her at everything. I doubt this, no mother catches their kids every time they do something wrong. It's just not natural.

Again, time to chapter. No, I'm not sure why, I just think it is time. Drivel needs many chapters to survive.

Chapter Forty Five – My First Stab at Parenthood

To have children, you have to get pregnant. I'm sure this isn't news to you. I told you several chapters ago.

I referred to belly as "Junior". I wanted a girl, so I was sure it would be a boy. This "Junior" thing was to prepare me for my disappointment.

I met DAD when I was pregnant with GIRL. We were friends. When my water broke I called the base ambulance to take me to the hospital, and I called DAD and his wife and told them.

There were two reasons to do this. First, the formal reason, he was my supervisor. He also drove me to work, since we were both going to the same place. This saved him knocking on my door with me not home. Second, they were my friends, I wanted to share.

In the hospital, everyone who visited who was male was suspected of being the father. DAD was no exception. We didn't know back then he would actually wind up being the father someday, you understand.

He and his wife took me home from the hospital, as well. They were good friends.

At any rate baby and I went home, we begin our relationship.

I was terrified. I had never even babysat a baby, never even changed a diaper. Now I have this tiny human being, and I am convinced I am going to kill her.

The Navy wives, they gave me their baby clothes they weren't ever going to use again. Several told me I could call any time.

Instead I would call my mother.

"Mom! She won't stop crying. I've burped. I've fed. I've paced, she's still crying. Oh my God she's dying, I should call the ambulance."

"Go take a shower."

"WHAT?!!!"

"You heard me right. Go take a shower. Whatever was wrong probably isn't wrong any more, now she is upset because you are. Put her in the crib, and go take a shower."

I am sure this is sheer cruelty. But I DID ask. And I HAVE heard before that sometimes babies have to cry. So I take her advice.

I only last five minutes in the shower. I can't take it any more, this ignoring this poor child.

I turn off the water. While I am drying off, I realize something. It is quiet.

So I go out into the room, GIRL is fast asleep. No more tears. Mom was right, imagine that.

There were many such calls, but GIRL and I managed. Once GIRL is out into the air, I am eligible for Navy Housing rather than living in this one room apartment, so I am put on a list.

When she was born I called everyone I knew. Her father I wrote a letter.

When she was 3 months old, he came to visit. He was transferring to a new duty station, so he had leave.

Let's call him, let's see, I know, we'll call him Joe. No, his name wasn't Joe, didn't sound a thing like Joe, but I'm not using real names, remember?

He comes. He bought me a frying pan. Nice.

He is here a week. He keeps calling our beautiful baby "IT".

IT is very cute. IT smiled, did you see that?

The night before he left I had him pinned to the floor, screaming at him. "SHE is NOT an IT! She is a CHILD! SHE even has a NAME! Don't you DARE refer to her as IT"

Perhaps this was my week of post partum depression, I don't know.

At any rate, I'm sure he was very happy to leave.

While we were waiting to see him off, I also saw Stephen King, one of my favorite authors, in the airport. DAD nudged me and told me.

"Very cool." I say,

"Well aren't you going to go get his autograph?"

"I am sure the man is busy. He is on his way somewhere."

Besides what would I say? First I would tell him who he is, which he already knows. I'll bet he even knows his MIDDLE name well if his mother was anything like mine.

Then I would tell him I love his books. Meanwhile he would be politely trying to figure out how to get to the desk before he is late.

Then I'd ask for the autograph. Why? Unless it is on a check, what does this do for me? I also have nothing for him to sign. I didn't bring a book or anything, I didn't come to a book signing after all.

So Mr. King was spared my drivel. You should be so lucky.

It is true though I love his books, I've read some of them several times. Now, before you think I will next be stalking this poor man, I read a LOT. I can't afford a new book a day. So I read them in a circuit.

I don't read all one genre. There is the horror, this is King's category. Also Koontz although, his aren't all horror. I don't know how to define his genre, so it gets thrown in there.

Next is the Classics – Wuthering Heights, for example.

Historical Fiction, another.

And so on. The only thing I don't read is romance, and I probably would read that if I was desperate enough.

So I decide which genre I am in the mood for, and I pick a book I've not read in a while.

The books I keep, like the Lord of the Rings and all, are books I CAN read time and time again. I don't have every book ANY of these authors wrote. Just the ones that I feel I can read more than once. Again, I am not rich.

Besides, you wait long enough, you can read most books again. You remember the story, but not the details, so it's like an old friend.

The really good ones you want to keep doing this with, over the years you replace them. Tolkien I've replaced three times, I have to do it again. This sort of thing.

So Mr. King, fear not, I'll not be behind you stalking any time soon, ok?

Don't laugh. He worries. He wrote a book about such a woman. It was even a movie. He worries.

I worry too. I think it's time to chapter again. This chaptering is hard work.

Prattle On - Teri Stricker
Chapter Forty Six – Venturing Out

By this time, you might be saying; "This woman has no clue what she is doing."

You are right. I told you back at the beginning about this. I READ, I'm not a writer. This is all Jon's fault. You should write and tell him he was full of beans. Except if you have come this far in the book, I'm sure you are just as silly as he is.

My mother always said; "Life is what you make it." I don't think she originated it, she just said it. She also didn't believe it. If she had, perhaps she'd have been a happier person. I don't know I'm just talking.

But! She was right, even if she didn't believe it. You have to see the funny in things. You HAVE to. If you can't laugh your arteries are going to clog up, I just know it.

We had a game when we took trips with the children. We didn't go on long vacations, but sometimes we drove places that were a few hours away.

So we rhymed. I love to rhyme, the kids loved to rhyme, and it stopped all the "Are we there yet?" whining.

DAD would join in, or if traffic got tight, then we had to "pipe down."

But traffic only lasts so long, after all. We could wait.

My purse has always been a place for everything. I had crackers and Kleenex and all those mother things. We always had something to drink in the car.

DAD was never one of those fathers who made you wait four hours to go to the bathroom, either. We were going to get where we were going, pit stops were not a problem.

DAD likes to plan trips. He does the Google maps, figures out how long it would take, adds time for leg stretching and all. He checks out the prices on hotels. This is even for trips we will never afford. For him, this is fun. As long as he doesn't pull out the credit card, it hurts no one.

I also always had a blanket in the car, and jackets. Even in summer. DAD never understood this.

"It is 80 degrees, we don't need jackets."

"Not now we don't. Things change."

Often we never touched the blanket or the jackets. But they were ready.

I get cold easily. The sun goes down, the temperature goes down, usually. This is a fact of life. I get cold, I tense up. If I get chilled, this is worse than just being cold. After a few hours my muscles ache from the shivering or the tensing, I'm not sure which. A jacket means I don't have to worry about it.

July, we are at my family's reunion. Well one of them anyway. They throw a party when my father comes up from Alabama to visit.

It gets chilly. I put on a jacket. Once I forgot. I ached for 3 days afterwards. So, the jacket is in the car, no matter how silly it looks in the hot sun right now.

After DAD listened to me whine about the aches that time, he doesn't ask anymore why I am putting a jacket in there.

Family reunions are fun. You see folks you haven't seen since the last one. When I was a kid, these reunions consisted of a lot of drunk people. This isn't the case anymore, although there is beer and all. Times have changed, and the people have changed.

There is always music and laughter. This is a good thing. You want crickets and crying?

There are a zillion things to talk about and you are all talking at once. Things calm down after a while, of course, you settle in and actually listen to what folks are saying.

I don't get out and see the relatives as much as I should. Most of these people see each other quite often. They talk about their jobs and the kids.

I've gotten to where I know all their names. This is a step up from my first one after six years in the Navy.

Prattle On - Teri Stricker

I'd look around and think who ARE these people? I'd recognize them, they had the family traits, the nose or whatever, but their names escaped me.

So they'd come up and hug me. "It's been a long time Teri Jo!"

"Yes, it has. Who are you?"

They knew how long it had been, some hadn't seen me since I was 12. So they weren't offended.

You go over the childhood stories. There are lots of people, and so lots of stories. It's great.

Believe it or not, I am the shy one of my family. No really, it's true.

My father and brother, they are social butterflies. They tell the stories and the jokes. I sit back and enjoy them.

I don't hide in a corner, don't get me wrong. I shoot out a one liner here or there. I am just happy to be in the background soaking up the memories they are sharing.

Before too long the guitars come out. My brother plays the guitar, sings some songs. Most sing along.

Then he wants me to play and sing. He wants me to take part.

So I play a few songs, I sing. I have written some about these people I love, and this is what I perform. Then I had it back to brother.

They like my songs and my singing. This is good for the ego. But I don't play much, because the fingers hurt, and I don't know many songs anyway.

I don't have to be the center of the universe all the time. If I am singing, well I'm the "star". So I talk and I sing, and tell my jokes.

If I go to listen to a friend, I can let them be the "star". They ARE after all, it's their show. I type a joke or two, this sort of thing, like any other audience member.

Some people aren't like this. Some have to be always in the center. My daughter was like this for quite a while. Becoming a mother has taught her better, though, I think.

So time to chapter and find out what to drivel about next, don't you agree?

Prattle On - Teri Stricker
Chapter Forty Seven – The DARK Side of ONLINE

In the online world, chat rooms can be good and bad. I told you there are people who come in to make trouble sometimes. People get upset. Why?

This is online, we don't know the people who come in. So why would it bother you that this person thinks you are a moron? It is obvious they are looking for attention.

The moderator normally gets rid of this person. But sometimes even a moderator has to go potty, or answer a door. So here they are.

"You are all morons. Sitting here talking about nothing when you can be doing important things" One said.

I am bad. I don't care at all what he/she or it thinks. I don't. But there is a logic fault here.

So, I answer.

"So, you are talking about us talking about nothing. This is one of these important things you are doing?"

Often, this is too much already, and they leave. They want to be king of the hill. They want wailing and gnashing of teeth, not a real live conversation.

Or maybe, they realized I was right, and went to find something important to do. I wouldn't hold my breath. More likely they went to find someone they could upset.

Once a man (well, actually, no way to really know if it was a man or a woman, but let us say man) came into a chat room to cause trouble with the name of "Shit".

Sometimes the names give you a clue before they ever send a line of text. He begins first by insulting my manhood. I have a unisex name, and he didn't bother to look at my profile.

So first I tell him he is right, it's so small it is non-existent.

The moderator of this room is away from the keyboard, or fell offline, or something I don't remember.

He goes on to the other folks in the room. Some are getting upset.

So I started a game. A word game.

"Come people, he is just talking. I like the name, 'Shit'. Let's run with it. How many phrases have we heard with this word in it? I'll start. He thinks he is Hot Shit on a silver platter, but actually he is cold piss on a paper plate."

They took up the game. We had fun. Shit left within five minutes, we went on for two hours. Why not? It was fun. He did us a favor. Conversation was lagging, now we have a topic.

Entertainers run into hecklers. People who can't just enjoy what is going on, they have to hurl insults. Generally, everyone else likes what you are doing. They are requesting songs, applauding, something to show this. So, you can ignore them or joke with them, it doesn't matter. If someone likes what you are doing, this idiot is not going to make them suddenly decide they don't, after all.

Most chatters are not the greatest typists. Plus, we are all lazy. So there are Chat shortcuts.

LOL – Laughing Out Loud – BRB – Be Right Back. This sort of thing.

When chat rooms were new no one knew anyone so the ASL (Age, Sex, Location) was asked a lot. There were no profiles to check. Some still come in a room and ask this. They are given creative answers or ignored. It is all in our profiles, if we want that to be known.

Chatter1: What is your ASL?

Chatter2: Well Chatter1, I am old as dirt, I haven't had sex since Jesus was born, and I am right HERE silly.

But you can also have good conversations about just about anything. The news, the daily lives of those in the room, anything.

Prattle On - Teri Stricker

We are all basically anonymous, after all. I can tell them how DAD or GIRL is driving me crazy, and they can tell me about their families. It's unlikely to get back to them, and you get it off your chest. Voila.

Besides, when DAD or other family members get on my nerves, they know it. I tell them. I am not shy anymore.

Online, just like offline there are all kinds of people. There are those who logged on after work, looking for a little light conversation.

There are those out to save the world through a chat room. This is where I get to tell them that doesn't work.

There are those who only go in to try to pull people into private chat to do the cyber sex thing. They think it is a singles' club. It's okay, we can say no rather easily. Although the moderator usually tells these folks it is not a pick up room.

There are those who are online day and night. They go to bed, leave their name in the chat room. I don't know, maybe they think we will talk about them while they are gone, so they want to scroll in the morning and find out.

Mostly I am in rooms where there is music, and the talk is all in text. I sing, I chat between my turns, I tell the current singer or player I like what they are doing. No biggie.

I also play games online. For some reason I liked online bingo for a while. There is a little chat window. We make fun of the electronic caller who is not letting us win, sometimes there are real conversations, just like other chat rooms.

So one day this man comes in. "So any hot babes want to chat in private?"

Hot babes. In a bingo game room.

I say; "We are all old and fat, and married. Perhaps you should try the VFW hall on bingo night."

Some folks had funnier answers. This is MY book though. That and I can't recall exactly what they said, so it is smarter not to say at all, you see.

Prattle On - Teri Stricker

Misquoting can get you in big trouble. And start rumors. And that can get you in trouble too. Trouble is easy to find. Oh. You knew that.

It is time to do the Chapter Waltz. Music Maestro!

Prattle On - Teri Stricker

Chapter Forty Eight – Work, and Calling Customer UNService

I hate having to call for tech support. I do. They have scripts, and they really HATE to leave the script.

So we got a DVR box for the cable. Very nice. You can record your programs and watch them later.

A week after we got it, it died. No time display, nothing. We hear a power hum but nothing works.

We turn it off. We turn it on. We unplug it for 30 minutes. All this we do. Nothing works so we call the cable company.

I go thru 14 prompts, entering my account number 3 times, so that when she answers she can say;

"Account number or phone number please."

Okay, so why did I punch this in? Obviously they want to keep me busy for this 20 minutes I am on hold, because otherwise she would have this information I put in.

I gave the account number again. Twice. At least she speaks English. Some computer companies, English is not their first language, and so you spend more time trying to understand what they are saying than on the actual problem. I spent minutes of time telling them the symptoms and what I have tried.

She speaks.

"Go into your menu and - "

I sigh. "Not to interrupt you or anything, but I just said there is no menu. There is nothing. I cannot go into the menu where the menu does not come up."

Now there is silence. I have interrupted the script, she is confused.

"Okay. Then please power it off for – "

"Excuse me. Do you listen to anything the customer says? I did this. We unplugged it from the power for 30 minutes."

"Please do it again for 5 minutes."

Great. So I go through all the steps I have done before, am on the phone for 25 minutes so she can come to the same conclusion I did. It's broken. We need a new one.

"Can I go to the office down the street and pick this up?"

No, we cannot. All the boxes like ours are on the repair trucks. So we schedule a service call.

"Now since all we need is a box, this shouldn't be charged to me, correct?"

"Correct. You will not be charged."

We get the new box, they take the old away. The bill comes in. $35.00 service charge on it. Plus tax. Everything in Tennessee is plus tax.

Another 20 minute phone call while we explain why we should not be charged for this. Every call you make, they take notes. Supposedly in our account, but they never have any idea what the last person said or did.

So if you wonder why I complain about service, this is why. They drive me crazy. I've been through customer service training, I know what it supposed to be done. This is not brain surgery.

It is the same if your Internet goes down. You call them up, there's telling your account number and all so that they can tell you there is an outage.

You needed to know who I was to tell me this? Is it a State secret, this outage? My old company, they had a major outage, it was right in the opening recording. This saved the customer time AND the customer service people time. They didn't have to tell each person individually that there was an outage.

Again, this is not brain surgery here.

Yes, I am ranting. It is very nice that you noticed. I smile. I do rant from time to time. Other times I rave. I've yet to foam at the mouth, but give me time.

Prattle On - Teri Stricker

My other pet peeve is unions. My father had the same pet peeve, and he paid his union dues for 20 years.

I worked for a big store. I had to join the union and pay the dues, although I was in the 90 day probation phase. Ok. Fine. It's $5.00 a week or whatever it is.

I am learning my job. Now when I work for someone else, I WORK. I don't sit and chat. I don't spend an hour in the bathroom, I do what I have to do, and get back to work. This is me. I've been the employer; I want to give them what they are paying for.

That's me. I was a stocker. I put out new stock. We had a quota to meet. They are very nice in the beginning, because you have to learn where it all goes.

I probably never would have made the 90 days as a stocker, because I fix things. I was always finding things in the wrong place. I spent much too much time fixing these things. You note it down on your form, but they expect a certain amount of time for fixing and that's it. They have to draw the line SOMEWHERE after all. But as I am a good worker in general, perhaps I'd have been put elsewhere in the store.

So you finish one job, and you can't find the supervisor. The others would stand around and chat until he found them. I would find a broom, and sweep. Or clean the fitting rooms. You'd be amazed at how messy people are. Their mothers would never approve I assure you.

The end of the night is the same thing. There isn't enough time left to do another department, so they chat. I sweep, clean, vacuum. I ask someone who isn't finished if they need help. This is if I've already called the supervisor and asked if he had anything specific I should do.

Employment is by sales. They have to cut back if the sales don't meet their goal. Last in, first out. Because of the union. My supervisor was not happy to get rid of me. He said I was the only person he never found just standing around.

Prattle On - Teri Stricker

My father used to complain of the same thing in his factory. He'd run out of parts to run through his machine, and have to go get them himself, because the person whose job it was to supply them was off somewhere. He'd get back with the parts; they'd be back, standing around.

I don't understand this. Standing around is boring. I'd rather be busy.

I am not a clock watcher. This got me in trouble on occasion, for clocking out late. I am punctual, punching in was never late. But I don't watch the clock. I usually know it is break time because people start passing me to go to break.

Watching the clock all the time slows the day down. It really does. I want that break cigarette an hour before break time if I'm watching the clock. It's much better if I am surprised by break time.

The end of shift is the same way. So in between tasks you look at the clock. This means sometimes I went 10 minutes over finishing a task. Oops. They don't like that.

They can change it. Most jobs, 10 minutes of overtime doesn't amount to much anyway.

So there, I have ranted. I don't know if it was funny, but hey, I got it off my chest. Time to chapter again I am thinking.

Prattle On - Teri Stricker
Chapter Forty Nine – Clothing. You Wear It Too, Right?

We've all heard about how teenagers know everything. We actually knew it all once ourselves. But then, there's the clothes.

No, I have pictures of my Dad in jeans, they were fifties teens. The greasy hair, the white socks, that was Dad.

The woman who swore I wouldn't wear jeans like a farm worker, she wore pants that zipped up the side. She never threw them out. She was going to get skinny again one day.

Forget the pants weren't in style. All women have several sizes of clothing.

There's the NOW clothing, these are the things we can actually WEAR.

There's the ones from when we were 20 lbs heavier, just in case our diet goes straight to hell.

If you were my mother, you had the clothes you wore before you had kids. These zipped up the side and were tight. She didn't have any poodle skirts tucked away, I'm thinking even SHE thought those were hilarious.

My mother DID lose the weight, but by then she didn't care. She was a hermit. Getting her out of the house generally required a pry bar.

In the sixties were the tie died shirts. My parents didn't wear those. My father had work clothes and every day clothes, and one suit. The suit was for funerals and weddings. Dad was a handsome man, but in his wedding pictures, he looks like an undertaker. You begin to wonder how bad he wanted to get married after all.

My mother was a beautiful little lady. I DO mean little. She was 4'11 ¾" and don't you DARE forget the ¾". Even in her "fat" days, she was good looking when she was sober.

I was a teenager in the 70's. We had the bell bottoms. Bell bottoms have come back with the name of FLARES. They probably have the same problem we did, do NOT ride a bike in them. The chain on the bike is hungry.

Prattle On - Teri Stricker

My class yearbook, all the girls had Farrah Faucett hair. Different kinds of it, but it was all feathered and it was obvious we'd made the best of our curling irons.

At my 20 year reunion we noticed this.

We had to wash our jeans over and over to get them nice and faded, as I recall. In the 80's they started doing that for you.

Okay, silly to want your jeans to look old, and faded, right? Wrong.

Now they have holes. They've ripped them and frayed them just for you. I've never seen the sense in this. They pay lots of money for ripped jeans.

Now also, the low rider hip huggers are back. I go through sheer hell trying to find a pair of jeans. It's all low riders and crop tops.

Folks, I'm 45 years old, I've had two kids and two surgeries, really, you don't want to see my poor belly button.

If you find normal jeans, then you have to find the right size. Men don't understand this. Their jeans have a waist size and a length size. Simple.

Women's clothes aren't like that. I wear a 4 in one brand, 5 in another. Or I did, anyway, I've gone up a size since then. Women's sizes have no rhyme or reason. It's enough to drive you batty.

Then the jeans, you got the normal jeans that aren't too low, but now you weed through the ones with the holes, the stone washed, the this the that.

Lately they have these jeans that look cruddy. They are that brand new blue color I remember, but then it looks like they were rolled in oil? WHY? Why would you want to look like you were working on the car all day and refused to change your clothes?

Then there's the bra thing. In my day, showing a bra strap was bad form. Now it's in. Believe it or not, it still looks stupid.

Prattle On - Teri Stricker

In my day the boys got all excited over a bra strap. Now they are everywhere. Oh well.

In my day? You hear this? I sound like my mother, my grandmother, my aunts. This does not bode well. I tell myself over and over I am not old, then I mess it all up with words like "in my day."

Then there are the bras. This was simple once. They were all pretty much the same. At least in my price range.

I am not overly endowed. Even after gaining some weight, I'm not. I don't even long to be. I need bras. I have to be desperate however, because I still hate paying so much money for so little material.

You have the padded, the under wire, the sports. You can crunch them puppies up to your chin so you have cleavage.

You wear these bras, taking them off, you have to be careful. I tell DAD to back away.

He could get hurt by flying breasts.

So shopping for clothing is fun. I am not young, wanting to show all my skin to the world. I want nice clothing that fits.

I don't want to wear jeans where breathing is optional, and I don't want them so baggy I need a rope to keep them up.

I am not fat. I'm not the toothpick I once was, but I'm not fat. I'm not matronly. I see the smocks and the shapeless things and shudder. This is what my mother's generation wore.

So I have this dilemma, you see. I still have a shape, and although I don't want to run around half naked, and trussed up like a turkey, I also do not want to look like my mother's generation.

Should I just give up and realize I'm old?

My mother was only 50 when she died. She looked much older. She put too many things into her body that said body didn't approve of.

But I am still only 5 years younger than she was the last time I saw her. She was older.

This wasn't just because she had the crows feet and the lines, and the gray hair. It's the MIND. She FELT old.

I don't. I don't feel sixteen years old, but neither am I ready to pull out the shawl and the rocker. So I am in this weird fistula of time, it seems.

In this place I like nothing out there they are offering me to wear. Well, again, not in my price range. I have tastes that are well beyond my thin little wallet I guess.

But these clothes I like, they aren't fancy. I'm not talking evening dresses here, I'm talking a decent pair of pants, and a shirt. This should not be so difficult, should it?

I've been watching people around here as well. People dress a little different in the south. The women are a bit, well, girlier. Yes, Microsoft WORD, I know that's not a real live word, I'm still using it. It's MY word and I like it.

The other reason I don't like tight pants is simple. I am a singer. Breathing is important when you sing. Taking in the air for a long note, you could burst a seam, you see what I'm saying?

So I have to take the time, leave the house maybe, and find some clothing I can wear without feeling like a freak. I'm sure it's out there. Somewhere.

Meanwhile we must chapter again.

Prattle On - Teri Stricker
Chapter Fifty – Good Health is Good

Another thing I have noticed, since I've aged a bit. I think more about health. At 30 I bought vitamins. They'd expire, because I wasn't taking them, and then I'd buy some more. The children took theirs, I made them. I rarely remembered my own.

Now, I actually take them. I also look at herbs. All that health food store stuff, I laughed at before. Now, I'll try it, what the hell.

I have never liked drugs. I take Midol and aspirin, if I need a stronger something, the Aleve. When I had oral surgery, I liked the Vicodin. First they want to give you the Tylenol 3. This stuff makes me sick. So I had the Vicodin.

I took it for the first day, then it wore off, and I realized, I wasn't in that much pain. Either that is just how long it takes, or I didn't need it in the first place. I switched to Aleve, it worked.

I am a smoker. I have bronchitis often, and always the smoker's cough in the morning. My nose plugs up etc. I don't take anything for all of this anymore. The antihistamines I take if I am so plugged up I can't sleep. Otherwise, no.

This is because I don't like all this stuff in my body. I never did. It's just as I got older, I realized that having the sniffles is ok. It won't kill me. Let the body do its thing. Its designed to do that to fight off the germs.

I don't go to the doctor for everything anymore either. I am sedentary in my job. I sit at a desk. So I get a pinched nerve every now and then. I know the signs by now. It hurts, it is true.

I used to go to the doctor. He'd give me the pills and all, after a fortune in x-rays to determine, yep, it's a pinched nerve. It would take six weeks to get better.

Then I changed jobs. No health insurance. So I didn't go to the doctor. I took Aleve when it hurt enough to talk me into it, and I went about life.

You know what? It took six weeks to get better. No X-rays. No hour reading magazines I care nothing for waiting to get in. So for that, I don't go anymore.

However, treating yourself is not always a good thing. For one thing, you have symptoms; you have to look them up.

This is when you learn you are a closet hypochondriac. It's true. You go to one of those sites and you look for your symptoms.

The problem is that something like a headache can be anything from allergies to cancer. It's scary. You start thinking you'll be dead in a month, a week, lord have mercy maybe TOMORROW!

Of course, this wears off. Hopefully.

Some things you find out, the doctors aren't going to do anything anyway. Like the common cold. There is still no cure. It makes you wonder just how common it is. But you don't die. You cough, you run at the nose, eventually you get over it. Whether you go to the doctor and spread those germs to thirty other people or not.

We want to go to the doctor when we don't feel good. We are damned angry when he doesn't make us feel better. But really, he is only a man.

He went to school after school, and for many years so that he can tell you;

"You have a cold. Fluids, rest, Kleenex."

Your mother told you this for free.

I had visions of the flu before I had it. I've had it once. I've also had one flu shot. Coincidence? I think not. I had a lighter version of what most folks get, but I'd never had it before.

I pictured this horrific vomiting and all, and basically when the whole family got the flu it was basically like a horrible cold with a full head. When people are sick they are as different about that as everything else.

DAD goes to bed. He asks for soup and water occasionally. I am the same. Except if you come in when I don't want something I tell you to let me do my dying in peace.

SLSIL wants to be mothered. If you are not in the room with him he will find you. Then he will tell you how sick he is. He is always sicker than anyone else ever was. But see how strong he is? He walked in here to tell you.

GIRL, she wavers between the "mother me" and the "leave me alone." So if you go to check on her, you aren't sure of your reception. As her mother, I've no fear. I tell her to pipe down.

When GRANDGIRL was just a tiny thing, before the crawling and all, the whole family got the flu. Except me. SLSIL is dedicated, he missed only one day of work. GIRL got it as soon as he was well enough to go to work and make all his co workers sick. Actually, this wasn't a big problem, security guards are usually alone, with a phone and a Billy club.

GIRL tried to be brave and all, but it never occurred to her to drink water. MOM didn't think to tell her, after all she was 19 years old and a mother herself.

So I came down to the living room to find GIRL asleep, baby in her arms, and moaning. One touch to her forehead was enough to confirm the fever. The chapped lips told me the rest.

So I scooped up the baby and put her in the bouncer. Bouncers are wonderful; I wish I'd had one for my babies.

Then I got a gallon of water, a glass, and the aspirin.

I woke GIRL and made her drink, and then drink some more. She said her head hurt, and she only wanted to sleep.

Basically it was like she was little again. So I spoke to her in the same soothing tone I spoke to my LITTLE girl in. You just do it, you don't think about it.

"Yes, your head hurts because you've let yourself get dehydrated. Drink. The aspirin is for the fever, take it. Then drink drink, and drink some more."

The GRANDGIRL spent the day with NANA, and we were the only two healthy people in the house.

I periodically went from bedroom to bedroom handing out water.

BOY is like his mother. Leave me alone. I was mean. "I will, drink this first."

So we survived the flu. I got sick a week later, after everyone was healthy. DAD brought me water, then left me alone. He's known me a long time, you see.

And also it is time to chapter again.

Prattle On - Teri Stricker
Chapter Fifty Two – All Knowing Mom, Sorta

Somehow, I don't know how, I have become the family Pharmacist. I don't understand. Even DAD comes to me when he has a problem and wants to know what to take.

I find it interesting. Why do I remember what is the best active ingredient in cold medicine for our family? It must just be that I am the mother.

It's built in. HA! I'm lucky I've not killed them all, I tell you.

However we had a puppy episode where I came out a hero.

GIRL and family bought a puppy. I told them from the first day they said they wanted one that they did not need a dog. Dogs require lots of attention, they need to be walked. They bark. The fleas, well cats have them too, I didn't mention those.

Several times I talked them out of the dog thing.. and then it happened. They got one.

Not just a dog. A puppy. A shit on the floor, chew everything in sight, PUPPY.

They had the dog house, the food and water dishes, the training pads.

Puppy went to the pads, they'd pick them up. Naturally, no pad, he goes on the floor.

GIRL would clean up the mess. After two weeks of this she is complaining.

I said "Well, where are his pads."

"We're trying to get him to go outside."

"So, when he goes inside, do you take him outside?"

"Why? He's already made the mess."

I sigh. "You taught him to go on the pad. Now you take it away, and show him no alternative. Is he supposed to read your mind?"

At any rate, this is a Beagle Puppy. One day I look them up. I Google. Hardest dogs to house train. Very smart, hate to be told what to do.

So not only have they gotten a puppy, but they've gotten the most stubborn breed. This is my fault.

I said once upon a time I loved Beagles. And I do. OTHER peoples' Beagles.

The puppy somehow got a banana peel. He got sick. While he is still running at both end SLSIL's mother gets ill enough that they have to pack up and go north to see her.

I have charge of Puppy. Puppy is now not running at both ends, but he is lethargic and won't eat.

I Google. Yes this is a trend with me, isn't it? Everything I find says "take him to the vet."

Yes, I know. If I had money for the vet, I'd not be Googling.

I did find a page on puppies that were often sick, and they had some hints about babyfood. Nothing else

Meanwhile the puppy is worse. He won't get up unless you make him.

So I close the Google and I think. If this was a grandchild and they had spewed from both ends, then got all lethargic, what would be wrong?

So I sent DAD to the store for Pedialyte and baby food. I fed him the Pedialyte with a tablespoon, then spooned some baby food after.

Two hours later, I still had to spoon the Pedialyte, but he wolfed the baby food. I kept this up every two hours until we went to bed at midnight.

I got up at 4AM and he very nearly knocked me over jumping about happy to see me. So it worked.

The GIRL and family return, and are naturally happy Puppy is all better.

SLSIL went to work, found out his friend took his dog to the vet for the same problem. $500.

I paid $10. So see, a little common sense, it can go a long way.

Of course, you don't let the dog get into banana peels, you don't have to do either thing. But sometimes things happen.

This was a case of a puppy eating food that gave him the runs. It was NOT a disease. If your puppy gets sick and you don't know why, you need to take him to the vet. It could be much more serious than our little crisis.

There, the disclaimer is in. I'd hate for someone to think I actually know what I am talking about or something, and kill their dog. I'd not like that kind of guilt on my head.

Time to chapter, I'm out of sicknesses.

Prattle On - Teri Stricker
Chapter Fifty Three – Nest Empty

SLSIL's mother was still in a bad way, and they decided to move to Michigan. We stayed here.

When you have two families living together your stuff is mixed. They'd spent most of their marriage living with us. Their dishes were mostly stored. They didn't have to buy towels, we had zillions. And so on.

We'd also bought things in the years we lived together, so the first part of the moving is determining what went with them.

This was mostly painless. We knew what was whose for the most part, and very little would have been worth arguing over in any case.

I have moved many times. I've gotten really good at packing things so they are all in one piece when you get to the new home. GIRL, well, she hasn't done this as much.

GIRL packed about two boxes a day. This means on moving day half the stuff wasn't packed. So this is all scooped into boxes willy nilly and put in the van or trailer.

The grandchildren are excited, they are 3 and 5. They don't realize that Papa and NANA are going to be far away for a very long time. So they don't understand the tears shining in our eyes as we put them in the van and hug them.

The first week is cleaning. They have left the puppy with us, so this is easier said than done. You'll be sweeping, puppy attacks the broom.

After 24 years, we have an empty nest. No toys scattered everywhere, no kids arguing. No turning off forgotten televisions at all hours.

It is very quiet. Except for puppy.

Puppy refuses to be house trained. I train me to take him out when he wakes up. Anything remotely in his reach is chewed. One of us forgets and leaves the bedroom door open, suddenly we see underwear running past us.

After the cleaning and the reorganizing, we eventually got rid of the dog. We are cat people. We are not dog people. I don't have the patience for a dog. This would be why we didn't have one before GIRL decided she had to have one.

But with puppy gone, it was even QUIETER.

This takes some getting used to. We had some milestones.

I took the child safety locks off the cabinets. I unlocked the dishwasher for the final time. I set my shampoo and my soap within reach of my comfortable sitting position in the tub.

Things I hadn't been able to do in years.

We were a little depressed, of course we were. So you have to look at the bright side. So, I would often say things like;

"Wow. I cleaned the living room yesterday, and it's still clean."

"I can run naked through the house now. I don't WANT to run naked through the house, mind you, but I CAN."

"We can have sex on the kitchen table. I don't want to, it's hard and uncomfortable looking, but we CAN"

So we got through those early days. We learned to buy less food. We are slowly learning too COOK less food.

We get phone calls every day from SLSIL. BOY, who I gave BIRTH to, he doesn't call, but SLSIL, at least once a day he calls. GIRL she calls here and there.

So we aren't yelling that we can't hear ourselves think, and we can't blame anyone but ourselves if we run out of toilet paper.

The stomping of little feet above our heads is gone, along with the scraping, the screaming and the rest.

We can go up the stairs without tripping over toys.

We miss the noise, the mess, the togetherness. We miss the grandkids coming downstairs to just cuddle, or ask us to watch a movie with them.

But we also enjoy the quiet. We are in that world of adjustment. We got married with kids. We've never been just a couple in our whole marriage.

Some of it is hard, and some of it is nice. Like not having to alert the media every time we decide to leave the house.

If we left without telling them we were going, soon there would be a phone call.

GIRL: "You didn't tell me you were going out."

ME: "Oh sorry. We are out."

Mind you GIRL and SLSIL didn't feel the need to tell US when they left, unless they wanted one of us to watch the children. They'd just go.

GIRL: "So where are you?"

ME: "Oh, didn't I say? We are out."

GIRL: "MOTHER!"

DAD is grinning at me. He heard that last yell.

ME: "Yes I am the mother. I am over 21, you don't need to keep track of my every step. Speaking of which what are the kids doing?"

GIRL: "They are – " crash in background. Sounds rather like a lamp. "Gotta go!"

So these calls, they don't happen anymore. We just go.

We haven't gotten used to it totally. We were all together, and now we are not. They are two states away now. The calls and the emails help, but it is of course, not the same.

However, there is also much less arguing, there's that.

And now it is time to chapter again.

Prattle On - Teri Stricker
Chapter Fifty Four – Stuff Needs Doing

I grew up, we had vinyl records. The 45s, the 33LPs. LP stood for Long Play. At least that's what Mom told me.

Then came the 8 track tapes. State of the art technology. That phrase gets men still, you know. All you have to say is "state of the art" and the guys are all over it.

Does he NEED to listen to 75 hours of music? Well, no, and doesn't, but this gadget DOES it and by God he is going to get it.

Tools are the same way. My husband has scads of tools. He has 3 hammers. He has 4 socket sets. He has pipe wrenches and doohickeys galore.

All this, and I have to scream to get a picture hung.

Okay, okay I lied. What I have to do is pull everything from the wall. Loudly drag a chair over to it.

Then I start rummaging through the sacred tools

He hears the telltale sounds.

"What are you doing?"

"I'm going to hang this picture of BOY."

"Why didn't you just ask me to do it?"

"I have. For six months. Now, I'm just going to do it."

So he does it. He didn't need the chair, didn't even need the small table away from the wall. I'm short, he's not.

This can backfire, of course. I took over the plumbing, because he didn't have the patience. He'd work for about 15 minutes and say "Can't be done."

This was then followed by. "Call the plumber."

I hate paying money for things I can do myself. I'm cheap. I might have mentioned this.

So I pulled out every tool to do with plumbing and started tinkering. Eventually I'd get them fixed. My brother he came over and helped with the big jobs.

BROTHER is a lot like me. We laugh a lot. Something goes wrong we laugh. Then we figure out what went wrong. Operator error, of course. The pipes, they don't suddenly change on you, after all.

We lived in a very old house, I told you bout that. We finally had to get a plumber in there because the vent pipe broke. UNDER the house.

The crawl space is not big enough for the plumber to actually do anything so we had to dig under the foundation and give him room to work.

The plumber would have done it at is hourly rate. However, like I said, I'm cheap.

So BOY and I are taking turns digging. I figure we will be done in about ten years, but I'm doing it.

DAD is working, making money so that we can pay the plumber when we can get him under the house you see.

In the midst of this BROTHER calls.

I answer the phone out of breath. "Hey!"

"You running the minute mile?"

"Digging"

"Digging?"

"Yes, you know, shovel, dirt, DIGGING."

"Did your cat die?"

"Nope. Tunneling under the house so I can get the plumber under there."

"I see. Why didn't you call me?"

"BOY and me, we're getting along. I save you for emergencies. You know, Bro, I call you daily for this crap your poor wife gonna hate me."

He laughs. We hang up.

A half hour later he is at my house. Digging.

I grant you he did it much faster than me. I do. I'm now useless, but that never stops me. I keep him company, I wear some dirt, I bring him things to drink.

He always shook his head at me when I didn't ask for help. I know this. I knew it then. However, I didn't like taking advantage of having a wonderful brother.

A house that old there is ALWAYS something you have to fix. No job is ever as simple as it seems.

I've learned since then, that this holds true ANYWAY. Any project, things are not the way they are supposed to be.

I'm not a carpenter but I know things are supposed to be square. And level. They never are. The studs are supposed to be "x" inches apart. They aren't. Multiply that by 12 with a house built at the turn of the century. Not 21st century either.

My brother and I put a new floor in the back room before we were done. This is where all the pipes came into the house. So you could now work on them from above. The whole floor was a series of drop in flooring. This made it easier, but if you DID have to get down there, you had to fold yourself in half. The joists all crossed in such away to make this folding in half thing necessary.

The crawl space had accesses, but that back room, it was an add on. It didn't connect.

So you couldn't just crawl from under the kitchen to it, you hit the foundation and said bad words about how you got all dirty for nothing.

Why? Why was all of this an afterthought? Well, the house wasn't built with plumbing to begin with I don't think. Probably not with electricity either. That was all added later.

The fuse box was in the kitchen cabinet. To change a fuse you had to clear out the cabinet. If it was the kitchen fuse that went out, you did this in the dark.

This is what flashlights are for.

See? Afterthought.

My husband did everything electrical, still does if it is needed. I do the furnace. He has this thing about gas, I have this thing about electricity.

I probably got that from my mother. She was always sure something was going to electrocute her. I just figure I haven't a clue what I'm doing.

You mess up a pipe fitting, you get wet. You mess up electrical, you could die. There's a big difference there. I'll stick with the plumbing.

DAD looks at the wires, and they MEAN things. I just see wires.

Of course, you turn OFF the power before playing with these things, I understand this. It still makes me nervous.

DAD knows how to do many things. Including the picture hanging thing, it's just DOING it. Once he gets started he loves doing these things as well. It's the getting started.

I'm like this too, otherwise it wouldn't take me six months to start to do it myself. I mean, let's face it, hanging a picture isn't exactly brain surgery, is it? No.

And so, it is time to chapter. This is because I am out of drivel about this particular subject. Yes. See you next chapter.

Prattle On - Teri Stricker
Chapter Fifty Five - Waiting

There are a million jokes about men waiting for women. That is not how it works in my house. I wait for the man.

DAD will say, "Let's go to the zoo."

I get the kids dressed, or when they are older I supervise. They get distracted easily. There is also the fact that they don't know where they stuffed their favorite shirt. They come downstairs.

"I'm ready."

This favorite shirt, it's too small. If they raise their hand to point, they are going to rip a seam. All the other mothers know about the favorite shirt thing, they have kids too. But I will still look like an idiot.

"You are NOT wearing that out of the house."

"But MOM it's the best shirt on the planet!"

"It's garbage. It's the best shirt on the planet two sizes ago. Change. Wear it tomorrow to dig in the dirt. Today you will look civilized."

Suddenly, I am my mother. Don't you hate that? First, you feel older than you are, sounding like your mother, Secondly she is right. No matter how old I get, I still hate my mother being right.

So they stomp up the stairs to change, wailing about how unfair I am, and again, I hear my mother's voice. "Tell him life is not fair."

"Life is not fair, my son, get used to it." One must obey one's mother, after all.

Meanwhile, DAD is working on the computer.

Daughter flounces down. She is wearing a dress. First, a dress is not terribly appropriate to going to the zoo. Secondly, I am killing myself trying to teach her how to sit like a lady.

"You need to wear something that is not a dress. You look lovely, but at the zoo, there are animals. There are dirty benches. Slivers. Go change into something you can sit down in. Jeans would be good."

"But MOM! I want to be pretty!"

"GIRL, you are pretty no matter what. I could roll you in mud and dress you in a potato sack, you would still be pretty."

"What is a potato sack?"

DAD is laughing from his computer. "Well, honey, it's –"

"If you take time to explain this, the zoo will be closed. Go change your clothes."

I have taken my 20 minutes to dress and gather all the accessories for the trip. The purse is bursting with tissues and other things a mother must have when on an outing with the children.

The children come back down, now dressed in a manner that won't have me walking four feet behind pretending I am not actually WITH these children.

Now I must get DAD ready.

"We are ready to go. Perhaps you should get ready?"

"I just have to finish this page."

He is a web designer.

A half hour later, it is now lunch time. I feed the children. "Hon?"

"Almost done."

"Uh huh. Well, if we are not going to the zoo, I'm going to have to break it to the children. It is now 1PM and it's at least a half hour to get there."

He grumbles, but closes his applications and heads for the shower.

By 2PM he is ready to go, we load up the car with things and children and we go.

Our day trip has turned into a couple of hours. We won't get through the whole zoo, but if I said, okay forget it, do it tomorrow, it would be the same thing.

I have had long hair most of our marriage. DAD, he likes his short. He's never been the hair down to the middle of his back kind of guy. I have no idea why he needs so much time to wash it.

Of course, he also usually shaves. I really don't think the llamas care if he shaves, but as it makes him feel better, why not?

After the first few trips, we finally learned to rent the big strollers. The kids are old enough that normally a stroller is silly. But the Detroit zoo is big. We wind up carrying them halfway through, because they are little, they get tired.

So for the first half we push the empty, rented, double stroller. The kids turn their noses up at it. They are BIG, they don't need a stroller.

I'm big too, but by the end of the day, I really wish someone would push ME in a stroller.

We enjoyed these trips. DAD and I loved telling the kids about things, teaching them things.

Of course, once they were teenagers, they knew everything and that stopped. Now they are grown, and actually call to ask questions now and then. They've forgotten to know everything.

Okay, okay I lie. My kids were not normal. They thought they knew much more than they did, but they did realize their parents were pretty smart. So I really didn't run into a whole lot of problems in the know-it-all department.

So there is our waiting chapter. Or whatever this actually turned out to be. Now we have to chapter again. This is working well I think, this chaptering.

Prattle On - Teri Stricker
Chapter Fifty Six – Christmas!

Christmas with a family is a joyful time. With children it is that much more so. The kids can barely manage to get through Thanksgiving dinner before they want to pull out the decorations.

To be honest, we were just as bad, though we usually did wait until the day after.

So you go into the attic, or wherever you store them, and you drag them all out into the light of day.

DAD sorts the lights, which are always a mess. It doesn't matter that they were neatly coiled and put away last year, they are still a mess. I think there is a Christmas light gremlin that lives in that box all year tangling them.

Or maybe it is an elf, because DAD does enjoy the untangling process.

While he does that, the children and I go through the garlands, which are also tangled.

Why do we have fourteen garlands? We have a 5 foot tree. Fake. I don't know, but we go through and gently untangle them. This naturally takes longer than DAD with the lights, because I have help.

You have different things to hang on the tree. DAD and I didn't like tinsel so much. It's messy, and we are perfectionists. Do you know how long it takes to put on tinsel when you have to put one tiny strand per branch? No tinsel.

The tree assembly the kids can really get into. The pieces are not easy to break, and the worst they can do is put the wrong size branch in the wrong hole. So DAD has fun directing them, and fixing the mistakes quietly.

Then the lights get lit, the bulbs checked. The children's faces are glowing. Oh I'll admit it, so are ours. We love this too.

Once the lights and the garland we've chosen are laced, now comes the balls and doodads.

Prattle On - Teri Stricker

We have the totally unbreakable things for the bottom of the tree, where Kitty is sure to bat things around.

There are stories to go with some of the decorations, and these are told as well.

Who puts on the star at the top, this can be traumatic some years, but we alternate kids. Looking back, I don't know why we didn't just put it up twice, once per child. But we didn't think of it.

Once the tree is lit and in place, you ooh and ah, you take pictures.

Now for the next month to month and a half, you will be saying "Get away from the tree" a lot. You have to vacuum around the tree a lot as well, not just because of the little pieces from the garland, but even the fake trees lose needles .. just not as fast.

A few years we went out and got a real tree. This is also fun. Everyone is cold, and rosy cheeked, and you don't care.

When you have children, you have Santa Claus. This goes without saying. I didn't make a big deal about Santa, but they quickly pick it up anyway.

So you go see Santa. The kids sit in the lap, you get the pictures, and it's all very nice. We enjoyed it.

Then there is the list. The list changes daily. My daughter's list was about 3000 pages. This wasn't because she was greedy; she knew she wasn't going to get it all. She just loved making lists.

DAD and I would look at her list. "What is this anyway?"

GIRL eyeballs it. "It was on TV."

"Yes, I'm sure it was. What IS it?"

"Um, I don't remember."

Ok, that can be crossed off.

My son sometimes had things he wanted, but usually, he didn't know what he wanted. He KNEW he changed his mind daily. He thought hard about his list.

When they are small it's even more fun, because you are writing the list for them.

"Time for the Santa list." I'd say and sit on the sofa with my notebook.

"YAY!" They'd run and sit on either side of me.

"I want Ballerina Barbie!" GIRL would yell

"I want TURTLES!" BOY would yell

"First, we don't have to yell. I am now deaf, I can't hear. Second we have to do one at a time, I can't write that fast."

So they'd settle in. And the list making would begin.

After the world peace and the getting the new puppy thing, we did okay.

Every year was the puppy.

"Santa doesn't bring pets."

"Joey got a new puppy last year" BOY would say.

"Okay, let me rephrase. Santa will not get YOU a puppy. See, Santa also knows parents, and he knows that Joey's parents didn't mind a puppy."

"What is bad about puppies Mommy?" GIRL would ask

"Puppies are wonderful. To visit. I love to visit Joey's puppy. I just don't want one HERE. In our house. For one thing Kitty would not like a puppy."

"But we could teach the puppy to be nice."

I smile. "Yes, we could. But we couldn't teach KITTY to be nice."

BOY is younger, but he already knows there will be no puppy. He remembers this conversation from last year.

So he gets a rather adult look on his face, and says in a voice that sounds rather eerily like his father "Can we move on?"

And we do.

You rarely use the list. This is just tradition.

You know the Superman watch will be broken before Christmas day is over, or it will be worn for two days and lost.

You won't get the makeup kit, you can picture it on the walls already.

If you actually spend time with your kids you know what they like, that's all. You know that GIRL likes Barbie and that BOY is into the Teenage Mutant Ninja Turtles. You know what games they would actually play and which ones would be too hard for them to play nicely.

The children went Christmas shopping with us for years, and never knew it.

We have a habit of browsing. There is a chain of stores in Michigan called Meijer. This has groceries AND non groceries. This is perfect for us. And their stuff was cheaper than the malls.

Today, you have the same thing with the Super Walmart. Same thing.

So browsing wasn't new, or unexpected. We browsed. We looked at what the kids ran to, and what they passed by.

A mere look to DAD from an item they spent time with would put it on the list. A tiny shake of the head, kept it off.

Sometimes the price was enough there were no signals necessary.

Once the list is quietly made, we step away from the children and look at it. We check off what on that list we are actually going to get.

Now DAD has to go to the bathroom.

"I may be a while, and I didn't bring a book."

Meijer also had pets. The gerbils and fish and all. So I would take the empty cart and the kids over there. This is a great place to distract them. With the animals and the fish time flies, they don't realize how long DAD is taking.

Meanwhile DAD grabs another cart, and plows through the list. He checks out, packs all these things in the trunk, covers them with a blanket. We had a Dodge Dynasty, this has a big trunk.

Then he comes and finds us at the pets, and we do the grocery shopping as usual.

The kids are packed into the car while DAD puts the groceries in the trunk. This worked for years. We didn't have to pay a babysitter, and still got the job done.

Every year we forgot the stocking stuffers. Christmas Eve we asked a neighbor to watch the kids and we race out.

Every year there is a toothbrush, toothpaste, and an orange. Then a bit of candy and little things. I tried very hard to limit the candy. They are really quite hyper enough on Christmas morning without 45 lbs of sugar coursing through their veins.

We come home, leave the stuffers in the car, and the rest of the night unfolds.

There are the cookies and milk. Isn't it interesting how Santa's favorite cookies are also DAD's favorite?

They go to bed. You know they aren't sleeping. You remember. You WERE a kid once too, right?

So it is midnight before you drag all the presents out of hiding and arrange them under the tree.

DAD and I know what we got each other, but these get wrapped too, because the kids feel we should have presents too. This is a good thing.

At 2AM you are lying in bed and you realize the stockings are empty. Those things are still in the car.

You nudge DAD and tell him. He suits up and goes to the car, you drag yourself up and grab the stockings.

By 2:30am all is well, all is ready. You can't wait to see their faces as they rip open the gifts.

4 AM, you are still awake. You know how tired you will be by dinner time, but it doesn't help. You're still going through everything, trying to make sure it is all perfect for your angels.

Finally you fall asleep and ten minutes later it is Christmas. This isn't a literal time period of course, but that is what it feels like.

The kids race into your room, forgetting to knock, and leap on the bed. "MERRY CHRISTMAS!!!"

We were cruel parents. Always we must have breakfast first. Looking back this may have not been the healthiest idea, since they rushed through it. They could have choked to death bolting their food that way!

So the rest, that's the easy part, you smile, you laugh, you break up the fight over the new truck. You eat until you can't move, and Christmas day is over.

You survived another year.

Now it is time to chapter. After all, Christmas is over.

Prattle On - Teri Stricker
Chapter Fifty Seven – Ice - Snow - BRR

Winter has never been my favorite time of year. I hate to be cold. I'm not real fond of being hot either, but cold is the worst.

This is why it is odd that I like to sleep burrowed under the blankets in a cold room. Or it seems so.

I have to be covered when I sleep, you see. My husband throws off the covers in his sleep if he gets hot. I don't. I curl up like a critter under the covers. If I am hot and throw them off, I wake up. I can't sleep. I don't know why, it's just me.

So snow is not a favorite either. However, the kids naturally loved it. The sledding, the snow angels and snow men. I had fun with them too, for a while, then DAD would continue the building and the angeling and I would go inside to the heat.

When your kids are school age, you have the snow days. Even when they like school they love to hear the newscaster say.

"No school, go back to bed."

Most of the time the kids were growing up, one of their parents was home all day. When the business went into the famine period of the "FEAST AND FAMINE" small business world, I would go find a temporary position, but DAD was still plugging away at it. And eventually, the famine ends, after all.

So on snow days it is now like a weekend. For Them. They don't understand the chores still have to be done, or MOM still has to go to work or DAD still has to help this customer.

So on snow days they hear "Pipe down!" a lot more.

Then you have to shovel the walk and the driveway. That is work. COLD work. Of course usually I did the walk and DAD did the driveway, but not always.

So I am a hermit in the winter. I go out only when I have to. The kids know this. This must be why they bring snowballs into the house.

"Look!" BOY will say "PERFECT."

"Get it outside." I say

"You didn't LOOK."

"It is a snowball, I see this. Now take it out before it melts all over the carpet."

"Mom they don't melt THAT fast."

"Ok. Take it outside anywhere. That's where snowballs live."

So he rolls his eyes and takes it outside.

That's the other thing. Snow on the boots. Kids rarely remember to take off the boots before running through the living room to the bathroom.

So you step in these icy spots. Even if it is just a wet spot, it doesn't feel that wonderful on bare feet.

I hear you. "Wear slippers." I do. But I don't LIKE to wear anything on my feet. I am home, I like naked feet.

These days I smoke outside, and I don't like winter any more than I used to. I put on the shoes and the coat and the hat, and then I take a blanket. I still shiver.

Now that the grandbabies don't live here, I could smoke in the house again, but you know, I've gone from 2 packs a day to a pack a day. If I come back inside with the cigarettes, then eventually I'll be smoking at my desk again. I know it. Then.. right back up to the 2 packs a day.

So I shiver and whine.

I would watch the kids go sledding, I wouldn't do it. I believe DAD went down a few times with them, but not me.

My son fell through the ice on the lake twice as he was growing up. Luckily, we live right by the lake so he didn't freeze coming home.

"Why were you on the ice?"

"Well because."

Great reason isn't it? Sometimes the because is more detailed, but, it amounts to the same thing.

"I've told you, that ice is never as thick as it looks, and even when some of it is, there are springs in this lake, warm spots, THIN spots."

So, off with the clothes into a warm bath. He never caught pneumonia, I don't know why.

I ice skated on that lake as a kid. I was stupider than my kids, and listened less. Don't tell them that for goodness sakes. I even fell thru once.... Only one leg, but up to the hip. It was not a warm and cozy feeling.

So I banned my kids from the ice. I knew the dangers. I explained the dangers. They still did it.

You want to follow them, and make sure they are okay. Make sure they are not doing what they should not, at least the dangerous things.

But you can't. You just can't. Even if you have all the time in the world, you can't. You have to let them go.

Somehow, some way, most of them live to see adulthood.

They try to build igloos you are sure are going to cave in on them and smother them.

They want to ride their bikes on these icy roads. Mine weren't allowed to do that. I am not sure they didn't sneak and do it a time or two after school when we were not home, but they weren't allowed. Nor the riding the bike at night.

There are reasons for these rules, but they are kids. Their friends do it, so they think they should. Don't let them. Be the parent. They live longer. You spend less time in the ER, it's all good.

So as I leave you in the ER with your kid who slid into that parked car, I won't say I told you so, I'll say "Time to chapter."

Let's go.

Prattle On - Teri Stricker
Chapter Fifty Eight – Spring at Last!

So, after winter, comes Spring.

Yes, I know. BOY said the same thing. "Technically, Mom, winter is the LAST season of the year, so spring is the first. So it doesn't come AFTER winter."

Yeah, well, yes it does. When winter ends, there you are at spring. So after. Don't confuse me with logic, it won't work. I confused myself too many years ago to fix it now.

By the time the snow melts, even the kids are sick of winter. Now we move to the mud phase.

Yes, wet dirt' that is called mud. This is what happens when it rains a lot. The dirty snow melts too, so now you have dirty mud.

Yes, I know, no such thing as clean mud. However, now YOU are the one digressing. For shame. This is MY book after all.

The first little bits of life burst forth, the birds come back and fill the air with song. It's wonderful.

Mud puddles are a child's best friend. They love them. The minute you aren't looking they plow through them. Stomping is best.

They ride their bikes through them as well, which throws water up and onto their backs. Also the mud.

The weather is not to be trusted. No garage sale yet, it could be freezing tomorrow. The kids are already clamoring to go swimming.

"The water is not warm."

"The water is NEVER warm. It's there to cool you off Mom"

"There is a huge different between 70 degree water and 50 degree water, trust me."

Of course, they don't want to trust you they want to swim.

Prattle On - Teri Stricker

By May they can wade a bit and chase the guppies. They are ready for summer and that last school bell, no matter how much they like school. We've been trained to long for summer I think.

At any rate, things bloom around you, everything feels fresh and new. Some things actually are fresh and new. After all every spring there are eggs in the nests and pregnant squirrels.

And the grass is growing sneakily. You are so relieved not to be shoveling, and you are busy planting your garden, you don't realize.

Suddenly you open your eyes and the yard is a jungle. Oh dear.

So the mowing season begins.

One year we lived next to a little boy. I'll call him Kip. I don't actually remember his real name, but he was younger than my children, and had the ADD. I was trying to clear the jungle for a few flowers. He is standing in his yard a step away from me.

"What are you doing?"

I tell him.

A minute passes.

"What are you doing?"

I answered him three times before I told him I thought his mother was calling.

"She's not even home. Babysitter is here."

"Well then I think she is calling you."

This didn't work. He was bored, not stupid. Darn it.

From then on I just ignored the incessant question. I'm a mother, ignoring children comes naturally.

Kip was maybe five, tops and forever doing what he shouldn't be doing. I felt for his mother, I did, but I also thought you should notice when your kid starts hiking down to the beach.

Prattle On - Teri Stricker

My kids and I walked him back home several times. A big body of water is not a place to be unsupervised if you are Kip. Kip wants to swim. He doesn't care about drop offs and cold water, he wants to swim, and if you don't stop him, he will.

I like children, but Kip was not on my good side. He drove my son batty, he drove ME batty.

He once threw a rock and whopped my son in the head. My son showed remarkable control in not beating him to death, I think.

So spring goes on, then you get to see the baby animals. They are very adorable, you have to agree.

You have to explain to your kids they are still wild animals and messing with them is not a good idea.

Even if the baby duck likes you, mother duck will not. She will protect the baby. This is nature.

My kids were mostly good about it all. That I know of, anyway. Once or twice I had to stop the duck chasing, but mostly, they were considerate children, even for the animals.

Now out come the bikes, they are oiled, the tires pumped, and of the kids go on them for another summer of skinned knees and ER visits.

I still love spring.

Yes you are right, time to chapter. Spring only lasts so long after all.

Chapter Fifty Nine – Prattling On

You look back, and you think. We could have done so much more with our kids. Hindsight is like that.

But we did spend a lot of time with them. More than my family growing up did.

We took them to the park, we took walks, and sometimes went bike riding all together. We were pretty close.

My childhood was mostly outside playing. I had a freedom I never gave my kids. Times were different.

Oh there were still strangers to worry about and all, but it was less likely. We knew all the neighbors, a new neighbor was rare. And watched.

I was everywhere but home in the summer. If my mother had known I went out on the lake in the neighbor's rowboat fishing, she'd have had a fit.

We got permission from the neighbor, and we didn't take it out far from the shore. This was a small lake anyway, the CENTER wouldn't have been far from the shore for that matter. If the boat had for some reason, sunk, we'd have gotten to shore just fine.

All the fish liked near the shore. So we were always just beyond where you could cast from the shore. It felt more like fishing; we got to be in a boat. We loved it.

But I was a careful kid. OR a lucky kid, I'm not sure which. There weren't a lot of ER visits for me. I needed stitches once. I had to get a tetanus shot once. That was it. I had the skinned knees and all that, just not the serious stuff.

We joked about my brother always needing to go to the hospital, but I think he averaged once a year. He just hurt himself in inventive ways.

I think that's where my son got it, come to think of it.

For instance there was a tire swing at the beach. Kids had swung on it and jumped into the water off it for a long time.

My brother landed on the dock. And broke his arm.

Goodbye tire swing.

He and his friends used to go down to the bridge and jump off. They were warned that water wasn't deep enough for that.

He didn't break his neck diving, however, he sliced his foot open walking up from the water to the bridge.

It's one of the harder parts of parenting, when your child comes to you bleeding or broken. You can't just make it go away, after all.

We had a great place to grow up. The neighbors were all close to each other, in fact if our windows were open, we heard their phone ring and went to answer ours.

But there was a small wood. There was a field. There was a beach. What more could you want?

Our road was relatively safe, it was a cul-de-sac after all, and everyone knew not to speed. Anyone that didn't belong on that road, they were also going slow because they were lost.

We rarely used the roads to go anywhere. We cut through yards, or went through the little woods.

When I say little woods, I'm not kidding. You could stand in the center and not be lost, because you could see the houses through the trees.

This is where we built our forts, and played with fire, this is where we drank our first beer. We didn't burn the woods down, whether it was because we were actually careful or just lucky I don't know. I don't remember ever having a problem and racing to put it out.

But mostly we climbed trees and built forts.

Prattle On - Teri Stricker

I hated shoes. I still do. My mother demanded I wear shoes when I left the house. So I did. I'd get 4 houses down to that little woods, and off came the shoes and socks. I stored them there, and ran off to play.

When it was time to go home, I stopped there and put them back onto my filthy feet.

She HAD to have known my feet didn't get that dirty with those shoes on. But she made me put them on all the same.

When you are older, then you have friends who want to be tough in the winter. They don't wear their hats, or their gloves. They are cool. They are usually the first ones to get sick that year too. Coincidence? I think NOT.

Germs make you sick. I know this. But making your body work harder to keep you warm can't help it fight off those germs either. That's a theory I have.

Not me. I hated to be cold even then. I lost mittens just like any kid, but I didn't refuse to wear them.

We had what we called an ice storm. It rained, and it froze. It was gorgeous. Of course, there was no school, you couldn't WALK let alone DRIVE on it.

Us kids all put on our ice skates and had a blast. Ice skating through your YARD is something you don't forget. We were all over the neighborhood. My ankles hurt for a week after, but it was worth it. I still remember that day with a smile.

The adults all bundled out and walked out gingerly into the yards and discussed how gorgeous it was, and also how they couldn't afford this day off from work.

Everything sparkled. By afternoon everything was melting, but up to then it was a frozen beauty. The TV told us some trees had gone down from the weight and all, but in our snug little neighborhood there was only the beauty part.

I'm sure some of the adults appreciated how pretty it was, but not like a kid does. A kid doesn't see the lost dollars, the project that is now going to be late. They see the sparkle. They see the shine. They put on their ice skates and make the best of it all.

When you have kids, some of that comes back. The butterflies are new and pretty, and funny again. The grass is softer than it has seemed in a long time. The noisy squirrels are wonderful and funny rather than irritating. It's the best reason I can think to grab your children and go outside.

Go. See what they see. It's marvelous.

When they've grown, and you start to get jaded again, then there are the grandchildren. You get to do it all brand new again.

But if you are wise, you can do it without a child in toe. Just step outside and open your eyes to the miracles all around you.

While you do that, I'll chapter. Yes, that's a plan!

Prattle On - Teri Stricker
Chapter Sixty – Ending This Prattle

This is the hard chapter. The ending. My life isn't over, after all. I'm going to keep working, and playing, and talking.

The various stages of my life, they aren't over either. I've just hit the "empty nest" stage, for example.

No pitter patter of little feet, no crayon on the walls, no irrepressible giggles. Well, unless you count mind. I tend to laugh a lot.

I wanted this book to be cute. Funny. I used my own experiences, because, well, that's all I have. I can't make people up. They wind up looking like a Picasso painting or something.

Some of the stories in here, since they are drawn from my own life, are going to have my family slapping me upside the head. "What did you say THAT for?"

Only figuratively, you understand. I left the sad tales out. The less than fluffy cloud stuff. I mean this is a fluffy cloud book, not an autobiography, or memoir, or anything so deep as that.

It wasn't an advice book. That would REALLY be bad. Me giving advice would be just plain wrong. We'd have thousands of white vans looking for us.

Although, you know, that could be good for the economy, right? After all, someone would have to hire all those white coats to chase us.

If you laughed, I'm happy. If you didn't throw it in the trash, I am thrilled. Maybe someday, when I'm rich and famous, you'll want me to sign it.

Yeah, right.

Oh look! A flying pig!

Well, he didn't really need to poop on me; I got the point before that.

So now I must set down my pen, or you know, in this case my keyboard, which, is already down. You know what I mean, don't go all logical on me NOW.

May your life be a fluffy cloud from this day forward. If it is not, keep laughing anyway!

WOW!

The End

Afterward Or Something

This book was never actually meant to be published. It was a joke. That's all. I'm no author. By now, you may have figured this out.

However, here we are. In print. Or rather in digital. I've become a bit more matronly looking, but the mind is as foolish as it ever was. The life keeps on moving' along. The family is still crazy, and I'm sure we'll stay that way. Crazy is fun, right?

I hope you understand, friend, that I don't know what I am talking about. If you don't know that, then here is your DISCLAIMER. I am NOT an expert at ANYTHING. Anything that sounds REMOTELY intelligent, it's an accident, okay? My OPINIONS. I fumbled through this book just like I've fumbled through life, and I've survived so far. That's all I know!

May the road rise to meet you, just not in the face. That might hurt!

Teri Stricker, 2012

Made in the USA
Monee, IL
08 February 2024